Foreign Currency Options

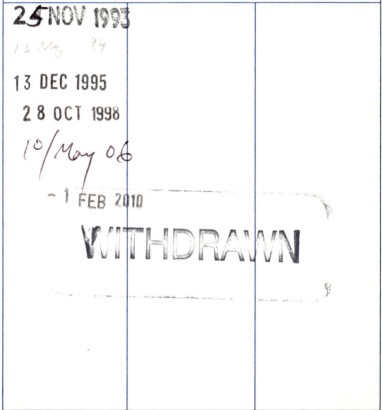

Foreign Currency Options

Robin G Brown

Butterworths
London, Boston, Dublin, Edinburgh, Hato Rey,
Kuala Lumpur, Singapore, Sydney, Toronto, Wellington
1989

United Kingdom	Butterworth & Co (Publishers) Ltd, 88 Kingsway, LONDON WC2B 6AB and 4 Hill Street, EDINBURGH EH2 3JZ
Australia	Butterworths Pty Ltd, SYDNEY, MELBOURNE, BRISBANE, ADELAIDE, PERTH, CANBERRA and HOBART
Canada	Butterworths Canada Ltd, TORONTO and VANCOUVER
Ireland	Butterworth (Ireland) Ltd, DUBLIN
Malaysia	Malayan Law Journal Sdn Bhd, KUALA LUMPUR
New Zealand	Butterworths of New Zealand Ltd, WELLINGTON and AUCKLAND
Puerto Rico	Equity de Puerto Rico, Inc, HATO REY
Singapore	Malayan Law Journal Pte Ltd, SINGAPORE
USA	Butterworth Legal Publishers, AUSTIN, Texas; BOSTON, Massachusetts; CLEARWATER, Florida (D & S Publishers); ORFORD, New Hampshire (Equity Publishing); ST PAUL, Minnesota; and SEATTLE, Washington

A CIP Catalogue record for this book is available from the British Library.

ISBN 0 406 10160 4

Printed by Biddles Ltd, Guildford and King's Lynn

Preface

The motivation for this book came from two sources. Number one, my long suffering publishers Butterworths who, when they approached me, thought they were just commissioning another book. The second, and perhaps more important, motivation came from my own inability to find a book which was comprehensible to someone coming to the subject of currency options anew in the mid eighties. That is not to say that I was unable to find some very good books on options. There are numerous learned tomes, but they either dealt with the higher mathematics of the subject or were exclusively dedicated to stock options, where of course the critical mass of the options industry was centred at that time.

I found that many of these books left a number of questions unanswered. Perhaps the most important, and I believe still unanswered, question is "What is the correct method/model to use to price options?" I found it rather strange coming from a foreign exchange and money market background where arbitrage is the cornerstone of the industry that nobody had set about describing the "right" method or model. After a fairly short examination of the subject and a considerable amount of discussion with fellow practitioners in the market, I felt that I was not alone in this belief.

It came as a strange sort of release a few years on to see an article published in Risk magazine entitled "The Holes in Black-Scholes" written by Fisher Black, one of the co-authors of the original formula. It was rather comforting to see Professor Black discussing the same fundamental points and assumptions of the formula. One always felt that perhaps the authors of the various formulae had that one hidden "magic" ingredient which one had missed.

What I have tried to do with this book is, by using a building block approach, to lead the reader to a point where he will know what to expect and where he will have to make his own subjective judgement. I would certainly not advocate options as the panacea for all hedging problems, judicious use is certainly required, but I hope that I have provided here an understanding of how the instruments work and what factors impact on their price. I believe that options are 75% science and 25% art and so, if after reading this book the reader feels that there are unanswered questions, I hope that he will see that these are the questions to which he must find answers. For example what type of distribution does this market follow? What type of risk reward scenario do I wish to use in my trading? Am I using the correct type of strategy to provide for the maximum pay back if my assumptions about the underlying markets are correct?

The one question which is most regularly asked is "If I write options and attempt to delta hedge using positions in the underlying currency, at what frequency should I readjust my hedge?" The answer to this question depends on correct assumptions being made about volatility (and the extent to which it is constant over the life of the option), relative interest rates and the way the market will react. I do not feel that it is possible to say that it is always correct to rehedge every move, or everyday. Neither is it appropriate to rehedge at every, say, twenty five basis points move in the underlying currency. In short I have not found a method which allows one to follow a rigid set of rules whilst delta hedging. Most of my colleagues in the market who attempt to delta hedge say that it is necessary to adopt a flexible approach and undertake some degree of under or over (anticipatory) delta hedging.

The introductory chapter which deals with definitions of foreign exchange risk is not intended to be more than a cursory glance through this most complex of subjects. I hope that my Corporate Treasurer friends will forgive me for oversimplifying what is an extremely complex task that they perform daily. Rather I had hoped in this chapter to give readers unfamiliar with the nature of foreign exchange risk an overview.

Listed exchange and money markets are constantly developing and if the information on listed markets is not entirely up to date, or the practices in the O.T.C. markets are not quite current, I hope that the reader will be understanding.

In the sections which deal with the Greek alphabet (delta, gamma, etc) I am indebted to Sheldon Natenberg, who is President of Professional Options Consultants in Chicago. Shelly is also an active options trader on the Board of Trade where he trades in the bond and grain option pits. If this were not enough, Shelly has also written a book on options entitled *Option Volatility and Pricing Strategies*. He certainly helped me to think through the segregation of risk in an option price and the subsequent management of that risk using the Greek alphabet tools.

Taxation and Accounting are always two very difficult areas for the non-specialist to explain. I have not attempted to re-write any information on this subject but have simply reproduced a feature from Futures and Options World which deals with these two subjects. I would like to thank the following individuals and their respective firms for giving me authority to use their work:-

Izabel Grindal   Futures and Options World

Eric Bettelheim   Rogers and Wells

Victor Levy
Stephen Kingsley   Arthur Andersen

Paul Dickens   Freelance Editor

It should be noted that no warranties are given as to the accuracy of the statements (either explicit or implicit) in this article or by reproduction here. Individuals and corporations should confer with their own advisors for specific advice. Further it should be noted that because of the lead time required in going to print, some of the information contained in this chapter may have been superseded.

The London Currency Options Market has in the past been likened to a club. I have always found the "members" most willing to give assistance to anybody who asks. It would be unfair to single out people for mention here, but this group have been of great value in providing a sounding post for ideas.

The Inland Revenue Press Release and Statement of Practice (Appendix 1) are Crown copyright and are reproduced with the kind permission of the Controller of Her Majesty's Stationery Office.

Finally, I would like to record my thanks to my wife Lesley and sister Helen who spent so much time laboriously deciphering my handwriting and turning it into a manuscript.

Robin G Brown
September 1989

Contents

PREFACE   v

CHAPTER 1   WHAT IS THE NATURE OF FOREIGN
            EXCHANGE RISK?   1

How does exchange risk occur? – ways of eliminating exchange
risk – analysis of cost/benefits using various hedges

CHAPTER 2   PRODUCT DEFINITION   11

If you trade on a listed market what are the governing rules? – LICOM
Terms and Conditions – margining requirements

CHAPTER 3   HOW A TRADED OPTION REACTS   16

Reaction of an option price to changes in the value of the underlying
currency – time to maturity – implied volatility – interest rate differentials

CHAPTER 4   CORPORATE APPLICATIONS   35

A comparison of hedging exposure with options, forwards and doing
nothing – matrix examples

CHAPTER 5   OPTIONS FROM A DEALING ROOM MANAGER'S
            PERSPECTIVE   47

Which currencies / maturities to trade – what are the objectives? – how to
control the risks

CHAPTER 6   TRADING STRATEGIES   68

What strategies can be used and what is the outcome? – calls – puts – straddles – strangles – ratios – calenders

CHAPTER 7   ASSUMPTIONS OF THE FORMULA   127

Black-Scholes – foreign exchange market random walk – calculating historical volatility – "fat tails" – put/call parity

CHAPTER 8   PORTFOLIO ANALYSIS   139

How do you manage a portfolio of options? – delta and gamma discussed – from today until tomorrow, and maturity

GLOSSARY OF TERMINOLOGY   157

APPENDIX 1   INLAND REVENUE STATEMENT OF
             PRACTICE   161

APPENDIX 2   INTERNATIONAL EXCHANGES   164

APPENDIX 3   FUTURES AND OPTIONS: A GUIDE TO
             INTERNATIONAL REGULATION, TAX AND
             ACCOUNTING   168

INDEX   195

Chapter 1

What is the Nature of Foreign Exchange Risk?

This book will introduce the reader to foreign currency options and advise on their uses and ways in which the attendant risks can be controlled. However, before embarking on the subject of foreign currency options, the question of foreign exchange risk is worth discussing.

TRANSACTION RISK

When an exchange of goods or services takes place between an individual or corporate body domiciled in one country and one domiciled in another, it is reasonable to assume that one of the parties will have to pay or receive currency which is not his domestic currency. This transaction in its own right does not present any particular problems if the exchange of goods and subsequent payment takes place immediately, because the party which undertakes the exchange transaction will be able to ascertain that the rate of exchange which governs the transaction in goods or services is at, or close to, the current rate of exchange. He can then cover his risk by purchasing or selling the foreign currency for his domestic currency immediately.

By its nature international trade is much more complex, often requiring one party to offer credit terms or to invoice in a third currency which is neither the domestic currency of the buyer or the seller. Once again, this does not present the two parties to the trade transaction with insurmountable problems, because in the case of deals which include credit terms, both the buyer and the seller can contract with their bank to deliver or receive the foreign currency at a predetermined time in the future and at a predetermined rate in exchange for their domestic currency. This will eliminate any exchange risk.

In the case of transactions which take place in a third non-domestic currency, even when credit terms are involved, the buyer and seller can contract with their bank to deliver or receive the foreign currency at a predetermined rate in exchange for his domestic currency either immediately (in the case of no credit terms being involved) or at a predetermined time in the future (if credit terms are involved). This will eliminate any exchange rate. This scenario is true for most major convertible currencies but may be subject to depth of the forward market or the lifespan of the trade transaction, but it is usual to be able to cover major convertible currencies up to one year forward. There may be exchange control requirements in some currencies which preclude these types of forward transactions or in the case of third world currencies no viable forward market, but bodies involved in international trade will be aware of these factors before agreeing to be invoiced in such currencies.

Tendering for an overseas contract

The example used here is that of a UK based company which is tendering for an overseas contract worth USD10 million with a period from tender to adjudication of six months and a current exchange rate Pound to Dollar of 1.80. For simplicity's sake, assume that there is no discount or premium on forward Sterling, i.e. US Dollar and Sterling interest rates are at the same level.

Tender price is USD 10 million at 1.80 = £5 555 556. When the tender is lodged the exporter has a potential risk for six months of USD 10 million. He can at that stage assume that his tender will be successful and sell USD 10 million in the forward market at a rate of 1.80, or assume that the tender will be unsuccessful and do nothing, bearing the full risk himself. Neither choices are satisfactory because he is unsure of the outcome of the tender and he is also unsure of the direction of the Pound to Dollar exchange rate. Therefore, the best he can achieve is to cover his risk. If he is lucky, he may make a profit by selling forward but not being awarded the contract. If the exchange rate goes in his favour, his forward contract could be closed out at a profit. Obviously there are an unsatisfactory number of contingencies in this transaction. At worst he will incur substantial exchange losses.

The following table shows the potential profits and losses under various scenarios.

A. Sell forward at 1.80 = £5 555 556

    I Tender is successful   Full hedge is achieved.

    II Tender is unsuccessful   (a) Spot is 1.80, he will close out with no profit or loss

                                      (b) Spot is 1.90, he will close out with a profit of US cents 10 per Pound

USD 10 million @ 1.80 = £5 555 556
USD 10 million @ 1.90 = £5 263 158
_____
Profit of   £   292 398

    (c) Spot is 1.70, he will close out with a loss of US cents 10 per Pound.

USD 10 million @ 1.80 =	£5 555 556
USD 10 million @ 1.70 =	£5 882 353

Loss	£ 326 797

B. Do nothing until he knows the outcome of the tender

  I Tender is successful

    (a) Spot is 1.80, he will sell forward the foreign currency at the rate at which he had budgeted with no profit or loss.

    (b) Spot is 1.90, he will sell forward foreign currency at a loss of US cents 10 per Pound

USD 10 million @ 1.80 =	£5 555 556
USD 10 million @ 1.90 =	£5 263 158

Loss of	£ 292 398

    (c) Spot is 1.70, he will sell forward the foreign currency at a rate which is US cents 10 per Pound better than the budget.

USD 10 million @ 1.80 =	£5 555 556
USD 10 million @ 1.70 =	£5 882 353

Windfall profit	£ 326 797

  II Tender is unsuccessful   Nothing happens as there is no foreign currency and no forward contract. No profit or loss.

The tendering company is, however, faced with a further dilemma. If the company tenders for a significant number of contracts and enjoys a low success rate, it would be nonsense to suggest that every one which is based on a foreign currency should be hedged using currency options. In this respect, option premiums could potentially prove extremely expensive. Commercial judgements will need to be used. It would, however, be argued that the tendering company will be best know its likely chance of success. It can then choose between the three alternatives, i.e. do nothing, cover and bear the full risk, or utilise options and establish the maximum degree of risk on the day the tender is lodged.

Issuing price lists denominated in a foreign currency

Price lists denominated in a foreign currency are normally issued and are valid for a six or twelve month period and sales budgets are compiled for similar periods. As in the case of a tender, the exporting company has to make assumptions about the potential future income, in this case, will sales meet budgets and in addition, will potential buyers seek discounts if the exporter's domestic currency cheapens in value?

Sales denominated in US Dollars are budgeted at USD 500 000 per month for the first six months of the year and the current Pound to Dollar exchange rate is 1.80 with no premium or discount on forward Sterling. The company issuing the price list is a UK company and therefore has an exchange risk for six months on USD 3 million at a rate of 1.80 (end December rate) = £1 666 667

A. Sell forward USD at 1.80   = £1 666 667

    I Sales figures are met   (a) Spot is at 1.80 when sales are made. No profit or loss as budgeted rate and sales rate are the same.

    (b) Spot is at 1.90 when sales are made. No profit or loss as rate at which forward sale is undertaken is same as budget rate.

    (c) Spot is 1.70 when sales are made. Opportunity cost of US cents 10 per Pound.

USD 3 million @ 1.80 =	£1 666 667
USD 3 million @ 1.70 =	£1 764 706
Opportunity cost	£ 98 039

In example (c), it is possible that the buyer might seek a discount because of the cheapening of Sterling viz the US Dollar. It would not be possible to provide the discount because the exporter is locked in at an exchange rate of 1.80. This could prove to be a problem in a competitive situation. If a competitor has not sold his anticipated foreign currency income forward for his domestic currency and could therefore grant a discount, this situation could lead to sales resistance in cases where a currency moves by a significant amount e.g. Pound to Dollar from 1.80 to 1.60.

    II Sales figures are not met (a) Spot is at 1.80, close out the existing forward sale with no profit or loss as both original forward rate and closing out rate are the same.

Alternatively, any residual forward contracts could be extended by means of a swap transaction to cover the second six months of anticipated sales.

(b) Spot is at 1.90, close out the existing forward sale, this will give rise to a profit of US cents 10 per Pound.

USD 3 million @ 1.80 = £1 666 667
USD 3 million @ 1.90 = £1 578 947
_____
Profit   £   87 720

Alternatively, any residual forward contracts could be extended by means of a swap transaction to cover the second six months of anticipated sales. This would give rise to the same profit of US cents 10 per Pound with the profit being realised when the original deal is extended. However, the new forward deals will be entered into based on an exchange rate of 1.90.

(c) Spot is at 1.70, close out the existing forward sale. This will give rise to a loss of US cents 10 per Pound.

USD 3 million @ 1.80 = £1 666 667
USD 3 million @ 1.70 = £1 764 706
_____
Loss   £   98 039

Alternatively any residual forward contracts could be extended by means of a swap transaction to cover the second six months of anticipated sales. This would give rise to the same loss of US cents 10 per Pound with the loss being realised when the original deal is extended. However, the new forward deals will be entered into based on an exchange rate of 1.70.

B. Do not enter any forward
    sales of foreign currency but
    sell when received

    I Sales figures are met   (a) Spot is at 1.80 when conversion is
    made. No profit or loss as budgeted
    rate and conversion rate are the
    same.

    (b) Spot is at 1.90 when conversion is
    made. Loss of US cents 10 per Pound
    as budget rate is 1.80 but conversion
    is made at 1.90

    USD 3 million @ 1.80 = £1 666 667
    USD 3 million @ 1.90 = £1 578 947

    Loss   £   87 720

    (c) Spot is at 1.70 when conversion is
    made. Profit of US cents 10 per
    Pound between budget rate of 1.80
    and conversion rate of 1.70

    USD 3 million @ 1.80 = £1 666 667
    USD 3 million @ 1.70 = £1 764 706

    Profit   £   98 039

Example (*c*) above is the opposite of A.I(*c*) and would allow for the offer
of a discount in an attempt to increase sales.

    II Sales figures are not met As no forward contracts have been en-
    tered into and no income will be rec-
    eived, no profit or loss arises.
        If sales figures are partially met, say, to
    the extent of USD 1 million the following
    would occur.

    (a) Spot is at 1.80 when conversion oc-
    curs, no profit or loss as budget and
    conversion are at the same rate of
    exchange.

    (b) Spot is at 1.90 when conversion oc-
    curs, there is a loss of US cents 10 per
    Pound as budget is at 1.80 but con-
    version takes place at 1.90

USD 1 million @ 1.80 = £ 555 555
USD 3 million @ 1.70 = £ 526 315
_____
Loss   £   29 240

(c) Spot is at 1.70 when conversion is made, profit of US cents 10 per Pound between budget rate of 1.80 and conversion rate of 1.70

USD 1 million @ 1.80 = £ 555 555
USD 3 million @ 1.70 = £ 558 235
_____
Profit   £   32 680

Again, example (c) above is the opposite of AI(c) and would allow for the offer of a discount in an attempt to increase sales.

COVERING BALANCE SHEET TRANSLATION RISK EXPOSURE

At the end of each financial year it is usual for companies with overseas subsidiaries to convert the foreign currency value of the subsidiary into domestic currency terms for balance sheet purposes. This exercise can mean that the domestic currency value of the subsidiary can fluctuate quite violently because of exchange rate movement even though the foreign currency value is constant or even appreciates. One method of eliminating exposure of this nature is for the parent company to borrow the equivalent value of the subsidiary in foreign currency, thus, the asset and liability will fluctuate at the same rate. (The following examples assume this is not done.)

In this example, take a UK company with a US based subsidiary with a value of USD 10 million and a last financial year end rate of exchange of 1.80.

A. Do nothing in the forward exchange markets between balance sheet dates

(a) If spot rate is 1.80 at next balance sheet date. No profit or loss because last transaction rate and current transaction rate are the same.

(b) If spot rate is 1.90 at next balance sheet date, there is a loss of US cents 10 per Pound, last translation rate 1.80, current valuation rate 1.90.

Last value of assets   USD 10 million @ 1.80 = £5 555 556
Current value of assets   USD 10 million @ 1.90 = £5 263 158

                                Translation loss   £ 292 398

(c) If spot rate is 1.70 at next balance sheet date, there is a profit of US cents 10 per Pound, last translation rate 1.80, current valuation rate 1.70

Last value of assets   USD 10 million @ 1.80 = £5 555 556
Current value of assets   USD 10 million @ 1.70 = £5 882 353

                                Translation profit   £ 326 797

These profits and losses are of course valuation of asset, profits and losses from one financial year to the next.

B. Sell in the forward foreign exchange market the foreign currency value of the subsidiary for domestic currency for the next financial year end

(a) If spot rate is 1.80 at next balance sheet date. No profit or loss occurs because the asset value in domestic currency terms remains constant on translation

(b) If spot rate is 1.90 at next balance sheet date there is a foreign exchange profit when the forward exhange deal is closed out or extended but a revaluation loss on the asset. This will give rise to a cash flow surplus but the profit and loss may not be neutral for tax purposes.

Asset last value   USD 10 million @ 1.80 = £5 555 556
Asset current value   USD 10 million @ 1.90 = £5 263 158

                                Revaluation loss   £ 292 398

Forward exchange deal   USD 10 million @ 1.80 = £5 555 556
Current value   USD 10 million @ 1.90 = £5 263 158

                                FX profit and cash   £ 292 398
                                flow surplus

(c) If spot rate is 1.70 at next balance sheet date, there is a foreign exchange loss when the forward exchange deal is closed out or extended but a revaluation profit on the asset. This will give rise to a cash flow deficit but the profit and loss may not be neutral for tax purposes.

Last value of assets	USD 10 million @ 1.80 = £5 555 556
Current value of assets	USD 10 million @ 1.70 = £5 882 353
	Revaluation profit £ 326 797
Forward exchange deal	USD 10 million @ 1.80 = £5 555 556
Current value	USD 10 million @ 1.70 = £5 882 353
	FX loss and cash flow £ 326 797 deficit

Those of you who are practitioners in the corporate treasury, foreign exchange and money markets will recognise these comments and examples as being probably over simplified and will argue that there are many techniques which can be used to eliminate or reduce exchange risk e.g. futures, internal offsetting transactions, foreign currency borrowing etc. I would agree with these comments and suggest that a separate book could be dedicated to hedging techniques. In fact, much has already been written on this subject. The above is an illustration of how foreign exchange risk could typically arise and some ways in which it has been hedged prior to the emergence of foreign currency options.

Foreign exchange risk defined

Foreign exchange risk is the risk which arises when an individual or corporate body knows that it has future income or expenditure denominated in a currency other than that of its domestic currency. If it then chooses not to sell its future foreign currency income or purchase its future foreign currency expenditure in the foreign exchange market in exchange for its domestic currency, an exchange risk has arisen.

Why would he choose not to cover this exposure?

There are two main reasons why:

(a) The exposure is of a contingent nature and cannot be covered without opening another potential exposure if the assumptions about the underlying transaction prove to be incorrect.
(b) He can delay the purchase or sale of a foreign currency if he thinks he will get a better rate of exchange because he believes that the currency involved will either depreciate or appreciate in value.

How does this all relate to the subject of foreign currency options?

Options provide the ability for the option buyer to purchase a contract to cover his exchange risk, whilst at the same time knowing what his maximum potential cost is. In addition, options provide the ability for the option buyer to purchase a contract to cover the exchange risk whilst maintaining most of the potential gain if a foreign currency appreciates or depreciates in value as led to believe it will. The three main choices open to the hedger of doing nothing, covering using futures or forward contracts, or utilising option strategies now provide the instruments to suit all expectations. The most efficient use of the various instruments is what will be examined in detail in this book.

Chapter 2

Product Definition

Perhaps the most fundamental characteristic which should be recognised about currency options is that they are a relatively new product and are very different from the old type of foreign exchange time options, which have been available for a number of years. The characteristics of this relatively new breed of foreign currency options are encapsulated in the statement: 'I own the rights as the holder of the option, do I wish to exercise my rights?' Whereas the old type of foreign exchange time option was where: 'I have the ability to choose the date on which I make delivery of one currency in exchange for another, but I must conclude the delivery by the final date'.

Today, the most widely used definition of a foreign currency option is: 'A contract which gives the purchaser the right but not the obligation to exchange one predetermined amount of currency for another predetermined amount of currency at a specified date or between two specified dates as determined by the option contract.'

Apologies are made at this stage for the liberal use of jargon which surrounds this subject. There is a glossary of terminology, which starts on page 157. The use of jargon is limited as much as possible, but you will find the book easier to follow if you familiarise yourself with the following terms:

CALL OPTION   The right to buy the underlying currency.

PUT OPTION   The right to sell the underlying currency.

STRIKE (OR EXERCISE) PRICE   The price at which the option is granted (e.g. USD 1.80 for GBP 1.00).

PREMIUM   The amount of money paid for the option.

'IN-THE-MONEY'   An option is said to be in-the-money if a gain is realisable when comparing the exercise price with the current market price for the currency e.g.

STERLING CURRENT RATE	= 1.85
STERLING CALL OPT	= 1.80
'IN-THE-MONEY' BY cent	5

'AT-THE-MONEY'   An option is said to be at-the-money if the exercise price and the current market price for the currency are the same e.g.

STERLING CURRENT RATE	= 1.80
STERLING CALL OPT	= 1.80
'AT-THE-MONEY' BY cent	nil

'OUT-OF-THE-MONEY   An option is said to be out-of-the-money if the exercise price is less than the current market price for the currency e.g.

STERLING CURRENT RATE	= 1.80
STERLING CALL OPT	= 1.85
'OUT-OF-THE-MONEY' BY cent	5

'OVER THE COUNTER OPTION' (OTC)   An option which is created by a writer to meet a specific requirement of a buyer which is not generally traded on the floor of an exchange e.g. Sterling Call at 1.8107 for settlement on 23 April and for an amount of GBP 207 501.00.

'EXCHANGE TRADED OPTION'   An option which is one of a series or a class of standard options which have predetermined specifications and are traded in a formal manner on the floor of a stock or futures exchange, e.g. IMM.DEC 1.80 call contract is an option on a future to exchange GBP 62 500 at a rate of 1.80 on or before the third Friday in December and is traded on the floor of the Chicago Mercantile Exchange.

If an option is a 'traded option', and this term applies equally to OTC or exchange traded options, it allows for the holder to sell the instrument in the secondary market at such price as is available. This procedure is preferable to exercise in the case of a commercial hedger, who purchased an option to cover a specific exposure and now wishes to cover that exposure in the forward foreign exchange market. This is particularly pertinent in the case of out-of-the-money options, which will have no value if exercised, but many have some residual time value, which can be recouped if the option is sold prior to maturity.

Much discussion takes place about the relative merits of OTC versus exchange traded options. Each have certain advantages over the other and, indeed, most professional traders use both markets and feel that they are complementary to each other. The following table will illustrate the main differences:

OTC Options		Exchange Trade Options
Wire and telephone market prices and trades will usually be discrete between the two parties.	Type of Market	Floor market usually conducted by open outcry. Some markets have a specialist system, others rely on locals and market makers.
International with no specific physical meeting places.	Location	Specific meeting place where trading takes place e.g. Chicago Mercantile Exchange, London International Financial Futures Exchange, Philadelphia Stock Exchange.
At the discretion of buyer and seller	Contract Specifications	Predetermined by a regulatory body.
At the discretion of buyer and seller.	Strike Price	Predetermined by a regulatory body, normally at USc2.50 intervals e.g., for Sterling 1.30, 1.35, 1.40 and for other currencies USc1.0 e.g. c60/DEM1.00.
USc/GBP 1 with no minimum movement e.g. from USc5.40 to USc5.41/GBP1	Premium Quotation for GBP	USc/GBP 1 with a minimum movement of 2 basis points e.g. from USc5.40 to USc 5.42 GBP1.
% of the US$ amount with no minimum movement e.g. 1.40% to 1.41% or units of currency per US$ with no minimum movement e.g. CHF2.00/USD1 to CHF2.01/USD1.	Premium Quotation for other Currencies	US$/unit of currency with a minimum movement of USc0.01 e.g. USc0.39/CHF1 to USc0.40/CHF1.

At the discretion of the seller	Currencies Quoted	Currently on GBP, DEM, CHF, JPY, CAD, HFL, FFR against the USD.
At the discretion of the seller	Periods Available	Quarter dates, usually mid March, June, Sept and Dec, although some exchanges always quote a one, two and three month option.
Two business days	Premium Payable	Next business day.
The contract is not guaranteed, the buyer must look to the seller for fulfilment.	Contract Performance Guarantee	Normally a clearing house is interposed between buyer and seller and guarantees the integrity of the contract e.g. CME Clearing, the ICCH, IOCC, or OCC.
Margins are not normally required, the buyer normally relies on credit assessment of the seller.	Margin Requirements	Margins are required for short option positions and in certain circumstances for long option positions. For more specific information reference should be made to the various exchanges.
Not available	Posted trade information and open interest	Usually available live via informations system such as Reuter and Telerate.
Normally the issuing bank will quote a price for repurchasing an option sold: alternatively the holder can sell a similar option to a third party and hold the long and short position open until maturity.	Secondary Market	A secondary market is available where a buyer can dispose of a long position and close out the two trades. Some exchanges have mutual offset arrangements where short and long positions exist on

		different exchanges and can be closed out against each other.
Normally all OTC options are options on the physical underlying currency	Options on Cash Positions	Are available on most exchanges
Are not normally available in the OTC markets	Options on Futures	The Chicago Mercantile Exchange provides for options which, if exercised, provide the buyer with a position in futures.

Chapter 3

How a Traded Option Reacts

Traded options are different from other instruments (be they ordinary stocks, financial futures, spot foreign exchange or interbank deposit rates) because of the manner in which the price moves. Normally prices for traded instruments are driven up or down by one factor and broadly speaking, this could be described as 'good news price up, bad news price down'. The situation with traded options is more complex.

There are four different factors which are all subject to change through the life of an option and will therefore impact upon its price:

Time — The number of days left to maturity of the option. This can only decrease until, at maturity of the option, the time value is nil.

The Underlying Commodity — The value of the underlying commodity can rise or fall thus causing the value of the underlying commodity element in the option price to react in the same manner.

Volatility — The 'volatility element' in the option price can rise or fall in value to reflect expectations of increases or decreases in market movements during the life of the option.

Relative Interest Rates — The relative interest rates of the two currencies in the option may change and therefore cause increases or decreases in the premium value. The 'interest rate differential element' is not a significant percentage of the whole equation but nevertheless will exert an influence.

The outcome of overlaying the effects of time, movements in the underlying commodity, volatility and interest rate differentials on one another is that a net option premium move (either increase or decrease) is achieved. Now to examine these four factors in greater detail.

1 MOVEMENTS IN THE VALUE OF THE UNDERLYING CURRENCY

If the value of the underlying currency rises, the fair value of the call option on the underlying currency must also rise, but not on a 'one for one' basis (at least not until the option is considerably in the money). The rate of change in the options fair value relative to the rate of change in the value of underlying currency is the hedge ratio or delta. Explained another way, consider an at the money option with a delta (hedge ratio) of 50%. If the value of the underlying currency moves by US cents 1.00, the corresponding move in the value of the option premium will move by US cents 0.50, i.e. US cents $1.00 \times 50\%$ = US cents 0.50. Therefore, the rate of change in value of the underlying currency will affect the option price to the extent of the delta, e.g. 1.80 call on Sterling with a delta of 50% and a fair value of cents 2.00.

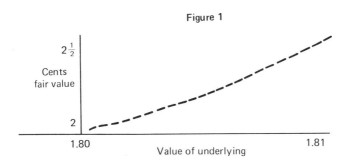

Figure 1

Cents fair value

$2\frac{1}{2}$

2

1.80

1.81

Value of underlying

Figure 2 (page 18) shows the delta plots for options of different duration.

2 THE TIME TO MATURITY OF THE OPTION

An option is a wasting asset and in the case of options which are out of the money if the value of the underlying currency, volatility and the interest rate differential does not change and, therefore, the option is worthless at maturity, the whole of the original premium paid will have to be written off (some of it may have been written off prior to maturity). The fair value of the option does not depreciate on a straight line basis, but erodes in line with Figure 3 (page 19).

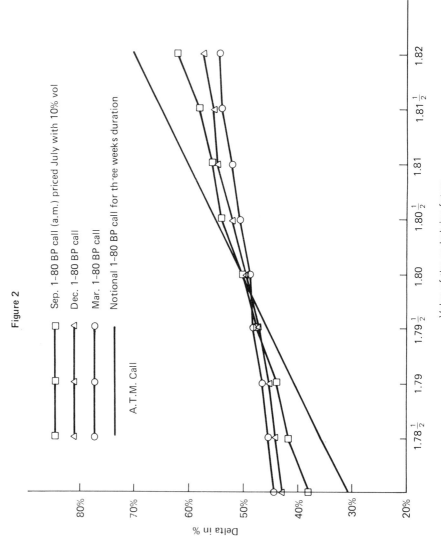

Figure 2

Sep. 1–80 BP call (a.m.) priced July with 10% vol

Dec. 1–80 BP call

Mar. 1–80 BP call

Notional 1–80 BP call for three weeks duration

A.T.M. Call

Value of the underlying future

Delta in %

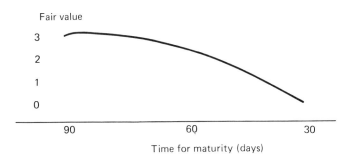

Figure 3

For options which are at the money in the final period to maturity this erosion is very dramatic, e.g. an option with a strike at the same rate as the underlying currency can start the day with a fair value of up to $\frac{1}{4}$% flat and end the day worthless (this does depend on the volatility of the underlying currency but is not an exaggerated example). See Figure 4.

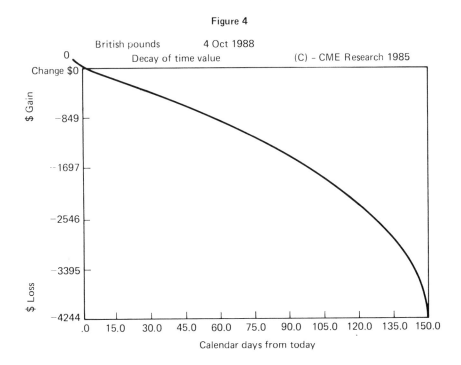

Figure 4

3 THE CURRENT VOLATILITY OF THE UNDERLYING CURRENCY

If the current volatility of the underlying currency (as measured by the annualised daily standard deviation) increases or decreases this will cause the fair value of the option to rise (if the current volatility increases) or fall (if the current volatility decreases).

Options are normally priced from the implied volatility of prices quoted on the exchanges, but it is reasonable to assume that there is a link between the implied volatility and the historical volatility of the underlying currency. If the underlying currency is not fluctuating, arbitrageurs will assume the risk of selling the option and hedge in the foreign exchange markets, thus driving down the implied volatility. The converse is true that if options are priced off of a too cheap implied volatility, arbitrageurs will purchase the option and 'delta hedge' in the foreign exchange markets, thus driving up the implied volatility (see also Chapter 8 – Portfolio Analysis).

4 THE INTEREST RATE DIFFERENTIAL BETWEEN THE TWO CURRENCIES

In the case of options on currencies with high interest rates or wide interest rate differentials, any large change in one interest rate can have a substantial effect on the fair value of the option, this is because the formula assumes a constant interest differential between the currencies.

Assuming that a call on Sterling was priced on a Sterling interest rate of 10% p.a. and US Dollar interest rate of 7% and either Sterling interest rates rises or US Dollar rates fall, the original differential of 3% p.a. does not hold and therefore the fair value of the option will rise because the negative cost of carry increases from 3% p.a. Similarly, if the differential narrows, the fair value will fall.

Confused? There are four factors all having a different effect on the cost of an option. The answer is to use a pricing model which will consolidate all the factors and provide a current fair value for the option.

An example of how this could work is shown below. Assuming that it is a 1.85 put on Sterling with the value of Sterling in the foreign exchange markets at 1.85, volatility at 10% p.a., the interest rate differential at 3% and it is a one month option with a fair value of $2.50. Assuming that the value of Sterling falls to 1.84, volatility declines to 6% p.a., time to maturity falls from 30 days to 20 days and the interest rate differential widens to 5% i.e.

(i) Fall in value of underlying currency = rise in fair value
(ii) Volatility declines   = fall in fair value

(iii) Time to maturity decreases   = fall in fair value
(iv) Interest rate differential widens   = rise in fair value

Expressed in cents per pound

	Original fair value	Cents 2.50
(i)	rise in fair value	Cents .50 +
(ii)	fall in fair value	Cents .60 −
(iii)	fall in fair value	Cents .70 −
(iv)	rise in fair value	Cents .10 +

Cents 1.80 New fair value

NB – These figures are approximates and used for illustrative purposes only.

Examining the factors which are included in the formula to obtain the fair value of an option and its hedge ratio (delta). These factors sub-divide into two categories, known values and value judgements.

Known Factors	*Value Judgements*
Currency spot value of the underlying currency.	The future volatility of the underlying currency over the life of the option
Current interest rate of the underlying currency for the period of the option.	The future interest rate of the underlying currency for the period of the option.
Current interest rate of the counter currency for the period of the option.	The future interest rate of the counter currency for the period of the option.
Whether the option is a put or a call on the underlying currency	
The strike price of the option.	
The number of days to maturity.	

Most of these factors are fairly easily understood. However, volatility is not a well understood entity and needs to be explained in greater depth.

There are two types of volatility, historical volatility and implied volatility which are relevant to option pricing.

Historical volatility

Historical volatility is an annualised measure of the daily standard deviation over a given period for the underlying currency. It is calculated by taking the rate of change for the underlying currency at the same time each day and measuring the daily price variations. The size of the movements can be logged and a plot constructed from the results. This plot will show the likelihood (statistically) of the size of daily fluctuations in the value of the underlying currency. This statement assumes that the near future closely resembles the recent past and, of course, this statement can be argued *ad nauseum*. For this reason, the number of days measured and weightings given relate to personal preferences and expectations of future movements in the underlying currency relative to past movements. It is arguably better to use a log normal distribution because it is illogical to assume that the value of the underlying currency can fall to less than nil whereas, at least theoretically, it can rise to infinity. To demonstrate this point it is difficult to envisage the US Dollar versus Sterling exchange rate going to zero, but it is possible to visualise a rate of USD 5.00 to the Pound (at least in theory). Thus when the plot is constructed it does not resemble a perfect bell shape but a lop-sided bell shape. See Figure 5.

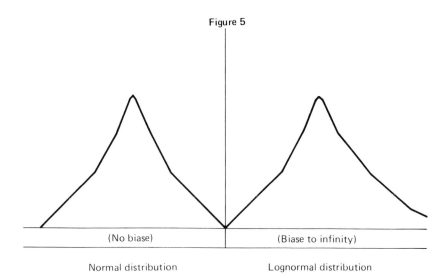

Figure 5

(No biase)   (Biase to infinity)

Normal distribution   Lognormal distribution

How then is historical volatility calculated?

Period	Price of Underlying	Price Change	$\dfrac{P_n}{P_n-1}$	$Ln\,\dfrac{P_n}{P_n-1}$	Average Log Change	Deviation from Average	Deviation Squared
22.7.88	1.7285						
25.7.88	1.7024	− 0.0261	0.9849	− 0.0152		0.0133	0.000177
26.7.88	1.6954	− 0.0070	0.9959	− 0.0041		0.0022	0.000005
27.7.88	1.7120	+ 0.0166	1.0098	+ 0.0097		0.0116	0.000135
28.7.88	1.7110	− 0.0010	1.0006	− 0.0006	$\dfrac{0.0192}{10}$	0.0013	0.000002
29.7.88	1.6924	− 0.0186	0.9891	− 0.0109		0.0090	0.000081
1.8.88	1.7010	+ 0.0086	1.0051	+ 0.0051	− 0.0019	0.0070	0.000049
2.8.88	1.6940	− 0.0070	0.9959	− 0.0041		0.0022	0.000005
3.8.88	1.6970	+ 0.0030	1.0018	+ 0.0018		0.0037	0.000014
4.8.88	1.6954	− 0.0016	0.9991	− 0.0009		0.0010	0.000001
				$\overline{- 0.0192}$			$\overline{0.000469}$

Daily standard deviation =
$\sqrt{0.000469/9} = \sqrt{0.000052} = 0.0072$

Annualised standard deviation (volatility) =

$(0.0072 \times \sqrt{252}) \times 100\% = (0.0072 \times 15.87) \times 100\% = 11.43\%$

Key to the calculation

Period	The period being measured. The table above shows a 10 day historical volatility using CME settlement prices on the near month British Pound future.
	For a weekly historical volatility insert weekly data. The number of prices entered will correlate the period being measured: i.e. 10 day or 15 week. Remember that you are not measuring intra period volatility but only the volatility which is calculated from the data which you use.
Price of Underlying	The price of the futures contract (or the underlying contract) which is to be measured. In the case of futures, for example, one could choose the daily settlement price.
Price Change	The latest price (Pn) minus the previous price (Pn − 1). It should be noted that this figure can have a positive or negative value. This is important because the next column uses an average of the log of this column.
$\dfrac{Pn}{Pn-1}$	$\dfrac{Pn \ (Price\ now)}{Pn-1\ (Previous\ price)}$
	The latest price divided by the previous price.
	An answer of 0.—— or less denotes a decline in prices (minus)
	An answer of 1.—— or greater denotes an increase in price (plus)
$Ln\ \dfrac{Pn}{Pn-1}$	Ln (natural log) of
	$\dfrac{(Price\ now)\ Pn}{(Previous\ price)\ Pn-1}$
	Then all the results are added together
Average Ln Change	The average of the natural log change, i.e.
	the result of the column $Ln\ \dfrac{Pn}{Pn-1}$

divided by the number of units in the column. Again it should be noted that the answer can be either negative or positive.

Deviation from Average

The deviation from the Average Ln Change. This figure is arrived at by comparing Average Ln Change with

$$Ln \frac{Pn}{Pn - 1}$$ (which is the log of the Pn + 1

actual daily change). Take care with the +/− sign, for instance Average Ln Change = − 0.0019

therefore: − .0152 deviation is 0.0133 deviation from the average, i.e.

$$0.0152 - 0.0019 = 0.0133$$

whereas: + 0.0097 deviation is 0.0116 deviation from the average, i.e.

$$0.0097 + 0.0019 = 0.0116.$$

Deviation Squared

The result of the Deviation from Average squared. The results are then totalled.

Daily Standard Deviation

One standard deviation is arrived at by taking the square root of the sum of the deviation squared column over one less than the number of units measured.

e.g. ——/9 =

One standard deviation =

Annualised Standard Deviation/Volatility

The annualised standard deviation is arrived at by taking the period measured and multiplying by the square root of the number of units being measured in a year e.g. daily to annual.

S.T.D. × $\sqrt{252}$ = Annualised STD or volatility

What effect do increases and decreases in the rate of change in the value of the underlying currency have? If the rate of change decreases from say cent 2.0 per day to cent 1.00 per day, this will decrease the annualised calculation of volatility (NB this is not a forecast of direction, rather an indication of the rate of change). The impact on volatility of one day's increase or decrease in the rate of change depends on the number of days used to calculate historical volatility and the weightings given. Obviously the shorter the period the more impact. Conversely, if the rate of change increases from cent 1.00 to cent 2.00 per day, the annualised calculation of volatility will increase.

Implied volatility

Most traders hedge options with options if they are managing a portfolio (see also Chapter 8 – Portfolio Analysis) and therefore when pricing an option they need to know where the market is trading in terms of implied volatility so that they can purchase cover for short option positions or sell cover for long option positions. The following table of middle implied volatilities from the Chicago Mercantile Exchange is taken at the close of business and it can be seen that implied volatilities vary from month to month and from currency to currency.

CME CLOSING IMPLIED VOLATILITY MID-RATE IN % PA

MONTH	BP	DM	SF	JY
SEPTEMBER	11.5	11.6	11.6	9.6
DECEMBER	11.8	11.71	11.7	9.8
MARCH	11.9	11.8	11.7	9.9

Implied volatility is calculated by taking the premium at which an option is trading in the market, i.e. the cost of purchasing or the proceeds received from selling a particular option, and solving the equation in reverse using all the other known factors, i.e. value of the underlying currency, days to maturity, the interest rate differential between the currencies, the strike price of the option and whether it is a put or a call. The answer which is derived will only be an approximation, albeit a good one, because one cannot be certain of the exact figures used for the value of the underlying currency etc.

The following tables show the effect of changes in the value of an option premium as a result of changes in time, the value of the underlying currency and implied volatility.

THE TABLE: CALLS AND PUTS

Futures Price	– Current price of the underlying in the futures market.
Estimated Volatility	– The traders' estimate of volatility which is to be used to calculate the theoretical value of the option.

Interest Rate	– The 'riskless' (i.e. US Gov't Treasury Bill) rate for US Dollars.
Expiration Date	– The date on which the options expire.
Theoretical Premium	– The theoretical fair value of the option as calculated by the pricing-code using the above futures price, estimate of volatility, interest rate and expiration date.
Actual Premium	– The price/premium at which the option is trading in the open market.
Implied Volatility	– The estimate of volatility which is calculated by the pricing model from the actual premium, the futures price, the interest rate and the expiration date.

It can be seen from this table that a modest deviation around estimate exists. This is caused by supply and demand but also as a general rule higher volatility is used to calculate out-of-the-money options.

TABLE: CALLS AND PUTS

Futures Price	Estimated Volatility		Interest Rate	Start Date		Expiration Date
169.50	12.0%		8.0%	08.04.1988		12.01.1988

	CALLS			PUTS		
Strike Price	Theoretical Premium	Actual Premium	Implied Volatility	Theoretical Premium	Actual Premium	Implied Volatility
182.50	0.84			13.51		
180.00	1.22			11.45		
177.50	1.73	1.75	12.1%	9.53		
175.00	2.40	2.45	12.1%	7.75		
172.50	3.24	3.25	12.0%	6.16		
170.00	4.28	4.30	12.0%	4.77		
167.50	5.53	5.50	12.0%	3.58		
165.00	6.98	6.90	11.9%	2.60		
162.50	8.64			1.82		
160.00	10.48			1.23		
157.50	12.48			0.79		
155.00	14.61			0.49		

Date: 08.04.1988 Contract: British Pound 12/88

TABLE: CALL DERIVATIVES VOL

The three tables entitled Call Derivatives Volatility show what happens to prices and their respective delta, gamma, theta and vega over a range of volatilities. For definitions of delta, gamma, theta and vega, see pages 65–66.

TABLE VOL A.   Table Vol A shows the effect of a lower than normal volatility of 6% per annum.

TABLE VOL B.   Table Vol B shows the effect of a usual volatility of 12% per annum.

TABLE VOL C.   Table Vol C shows the effect of a higher than average volatility of 18% per annum.

All examples use a constant future of $1.69\frac{1}{2}$, interest rate of 8%, start date of 1 August and expiration date of 1 December.

TABLE: CALL DERIVATIVES VOL A

Futures Price	Estimated Volatility	Interest Rate	Start Date	Expiration Date
169.50	6.0%	8.0%	08.01.1988	12.01.1988

Derivatives

Strike Price	Theoretical Premium	Delta	Gamma	Theta	Vega
182.50	0.04	1.7%	0.7%	0.001	0.041
180.00	0.10	4.2%	1.5%	0.002	0.087
177.50	0.25	9.2%	2.8%	0.004	0.161
175.00	0.56	17.8%	4.4%	0.006	0.253
172.50	1.13	30.4%	5.9%	0.008	0.338
170.00	2.05	46.1%	6.6%	0.009	0.380
167.50	3.37	62.3%	6.2%	0.009	0.357
165.00	5.09	76.5%	4.8%	0.007	0.278
162.50	7.12	86.8%	3.1%	0.004	0.178
160.00	9.50	92.8%	1.6%	0.002	0.093
157.50	12.00	95.8%	0.7%	0.001	0.039
155.00	14.50	96.9%	0.2%	0.000	0.013

Date: 08.01.1988   Contract: British Pound 12/88

TABLE: CALL DERIVATIVES VOL B

Futures Price 169.50	*Estimated Volatility* 12.0%	*Interest Rate* 8.0%	*Start Date* 08.01.1988	*Expiration Date* 12.01.1988

Derivatives

Strike Price	*Theoretical Premium*	*Delta*	*Gamma*	*Theta*	*Vega*
182.50	0.87	14.7%	1.9%	0.011	0.224
180.00	1.26	19.7%	2.3%	0.013	0.269
177.50	1.78	25.7%	2.7%	0.015	0.312
175.00	2.45	32.6%	3.0%	0.017	0.348
172.50	3.29	40.3%	3.2%	0.018	0.372
170.00	4.34	48.4%	3.3%	0.019	0.381
167.50	5.58	56.6%	3.2%	0.018	0.373
165.00	7.03	64.6%	3.0%	0.017	0.348
162.50	8.68	72.0%	2.7%	0.015	0.310
160.00	10.51	78.5%	2.3%	0.013	0.262
157.50	12.51	84.0%	1.8%	0.010	0.209
155.00	14.63	88.3%	1.4%	0.008	0.158

Date: 08.01.1988   Contract: British Pound 12/88

TABLE: CALL DERIVATIVES VOL C

Futures Price 169.50	*Estimated Volatility* 18.0%	*Interest Rate* 8.0%	*Start Date* 08.01.1988	*Expiration Date* 12.01.1988

Derivatives

Strike Price	*Theoretical Premium*	*Delta*	*Gamma*	*Theta*	*Vega*
182.50	2.50	24.9%	1.8%	0.023	0.307
180.00	3.09	29.2%	1.9%	0.024	0.332
177.50	3.79	33.9%	2.0%	0.026	0.353
175.00	4.61	38.9%	2.1%	0.027	0.368
172.50	5.55	44.2%	2.2%	0.028	0.378
170.00	6.62	49.6%	2.2%	0.028	0.381
167.50	7.83	55.1%	2.2%	0.028	0.375
165.00	9.17	60.6%	2.1%	0.027	0.363
162.50	10.66	65.8%	2.0%	0.025	0.343
160.00	12.28	70.9%	1.8%	0.023	0.317
157.50	14.03	75.5%	1.7%	0.021	0.286
155.00	15.89	79.7%	1.5%	0.019	0.251

Date: 08.01.1988   Contract: British Pound 12/88

TABLE: CALL DERIVATIVES TIME

The four tables entitled Call Derivatives Time show what happens as a result of the progression of time.

Table A shows the derivatives when the option starts on 4 August. Table B starts on 1 September. Table C starts on 3 October and finally Table D shows the start on 1 November.

All examples use a constant future of $1.69\frac{1}{2}$, interest rate 8%, final date of 1 December and a volatility of 12%

TABLE: CALL DERIVATIVES TIME A

Futures Price	Estimated Volatility	Interest Rate	Start Date	Expiration Date
169.50	12.0%	8.0%	08.04.1988	12.01.1988

Derivatives

Strike Price	Theoretical Premium	Delta	Gamma	Theta	Vega
182.50	0.84	14.4%	1.9%	0.011	0.218
180.00	1.22	19.4%	2.3%	0.013	0.264
177.50	1.73	25.5%	2.7%	0.015	0.307
175.00	2.40	32.4%	3.0%	0.017	0.343
172.50	3.24	40.2%	3.3%	0.019	0.367
170.00	4.28	48.4%	3.3%	0.019	0.376
167.50	5.53	56.7%	3.3%	0.019	0.368
165.00	6.98	64.8%	3.1%	0.017	0.343
162.50	8.64	72.3%	2.7%	0.015	0.305
160.00	10.48	78.9%	2.3%	0.013	0.256
157.50	12.48	84.3%	1.8%	0.010	0.204
155.00	14.61	88.6%	1.4%	0.008	0.153

Date: 08.04.1988   Contract: British Pound 12/88

TABLE: CALL DERIVATIVES TIME B

Futures Price	Estimated Volatility	Interest Rate	Start Date	Expiration Date
169.50	12.0%	8.0%	09.01.1988	12.01.1988

Derivatives

Strike Price	Theoretical Premium	Delta	Gamma	Theta	Vega
182.50	0.54	11.2%	1.9%	0.011	0.160
180.00	0.85	16.2%	2.4%	0.014	0.206
177.50	1.29	22.5%	2.9%	0.017	0.252
175.00	1.90	30.1%	3.4%	0.019	0.292
172.50	2.71	38.9%	3.7%	0.021	0.320
170.00	3.74	48.3%	3.8%	0.022	0.331
167.50	5.00	57.9%	3.8%	0.021	0.322
165.00	6.51	67.1%	3.4%	0.019	0.295
162.50	8.25	75.3%	2.9%	0.017	0.253
160.00	10.18	82.3%	2.4%	0.013	0.202
157.50	12.27	87.8%	1.8%	0.010	0.151
155.00	14.50	91.8%	1.2%	0.007	0.104

Date: 09.01.1988   Contract: British Pound 12/88

TABLE: CALL DERIVATIVES TIME C

Futures Price	Estimated Volatility	Interest Rate	Start Date	Expiration Date
169.50	12.0%	8.0%	10.03.1988	12.01.1988

Derivatives

Strike Price	Theoretical Premium	Delta	Gamma	Theta	Vega
182.50	0.23	6.5%	1.5%	0.009	0.086
180.00	0.42	10.9%	2.3%	0.013	0.127
177.50	0.75	17.3%	3.1%	0.018	0.174
175.00	1.25	25.8%	3.9%	0.022	0.219
172.50	1.98	36.2%	4.5%	0.026	0.253
170.00	2.98	47.9%	4.8%	0.027	0.268
167.50	4.28	59.9%	4.6%	0.026	0.259
165.00	5.88	71.0%	4.1%	0.023	0.227
162.50	7.74	80.5%	3.2%	0.018	0.179
160.00	9.82	87.7%	2.3%	0.013	0.128
157.50	12.06	92.7%	1.5%	0.008	0.081
155.00	14.50	95.7%	0.8%	0.005	0.046

Date: 10.03.1988   Contract: British Pound 12/88

TABLE: CALL DERIVATIVES TIME D

Futures Price	Estimated Volatility	Interest Rate	Start Date	Expiration Date
169.50	12.0%	8.0%	11.01.1988	12.01.1988

Derivatives

Strike Price	Theoretical Premium	Delta	Gamma	Theta	Vega
182.50	0.03	1.6%	0.7%	0.004	0.020
180.00	0.10	4.2%	1.5%	0.009	0.043
177.50	0.25	9.2%	2.8%	0.016	0.080
175.00	0.56	18.0%	4.5%	0.025	0.127
172.50	1.14	30.9%	6.0%	0.034	0.171
170.00	2.07	47.0%	6.8%	0.038	0.192
167.50	3.43	63.7%	6.4%	0.036	0.180
165.00	5.18	78.3%	4.9%	0.028	0.140
162.50	7.26	88.7%	3.1%	0.018	0.089
160.00	9.55	94.9%	1.6%	0.009	0.046
157.50	12.00	97.8%	0.7%	0.004	0.019
155.00	14.50	98.9%	0.2%	0.001	0.006

Date: 11.01.1988   Contract: British Pound 12/88

DAY TRADER SHEET

The day trader shows the effect of changes in the option premium and their respective deltas for changes in the value of the underlying futures contract.

The print out assumes a futures price of 1.6950, volatility of 12%, an interest rate of 8%, a start date of 1 August, with an expiration date of 1 December.

DAY TRADE SHEET

Black model option premiums and deltas at different futures price

Futures Price 169.50	Estimated Volatility 12.0%		Interest Rate 8.0%		Start Date 08.01.1988			Expiration Date 12.01.1988	
FUTURES PRICES					STRIKE PRICES				
	160.00	162.50	165.00	167.50	170.00	172.50	175.00	177.50	180.00
170.50 Calls	11.31	9.42	7.69	6.16	4.84	3.71	2.79	2.05	1.47
Deltas	80.7%	74.6%	67.6%	59.8%	51.7%	43.5%	35.7%	28.5%	22.2%
Puts	1.09	1.63	2.34	3.24	4.35	5.66	7.17	8.86	10.72
Deltas	16.6%	22.7%	29.8%	37.6%	45.7%	53.8%	61.7%	68.9%	75.2%
170.25 Calls	11.11	9.23	7.52	6.01	4.71	3.60	2.70	1.98	1.41
Deltas	80.2%	74.0%	66.8%	59.0%	50.9%	42.7%	34.9%	27.8%	21.5%
Puts	1.13	1.68	2.41	3.33	4.46	5.79	7.32	9.04	10.91
Deltas	17.2%	23.4%	30.5%	38.3%	46.5%	54.7%	62.4%	69.6%	75.8%
170.00 Calls	10.91	9.05	7.36	5.87	4.58	3.50	2.61	1.91	1.36
Deltas	79.7%	73.3%	66.1%	58.2%	50.0%	41.9%	34.2%	27.1%	20.9%
Puts	1.17	1.74	2.49	3.43	4.58	5.93	7.48	9.21	11.10
Deltas	17.7%	24.0%	31.3%	39.1%	47.3%	55.5%	63.2%	70.3%	76.4%
169.75 Calls	10.71	8.86	7.19	5.72	4.46	3.39	2.53	1.84	1.31
Deltas	79.1%	72.7%	65.4%	57.4%	49.2%	41.1%	33.4%	26.4%	20.3%
Puts	1.22	1.80	2.57	3.53	4.70	6.07	7.64	9.39	11.29
Deltas	18.3%	24.7%	32.0%	39.9%	48.2%	56.3%	64.0%	70.9%	77.0%

169.50 Calls	10.51	8.68	7.03	5.58	4.34	3.29	2.45	1.78	1.26
Deltas	78.5%	72.0%	64.6%	56.6%	48.4%	40.3%	32.6%	25.7%	19.7%
Puts	1.26	1.87	2.65	3.63	4.82	6.21	7.80	9.56	11.48
Deltas	18.8%	25.3%	32.7%	40.6%	49.0%	57.1%	64.7%	71.6%	77.6%
169.25 Calls	10.32	8.50	6.87	5.44	4.21	3.19	2.37	1.71	1.21
Deltas	78.0%	71.3%	63.9%	55.8%	47.6%	39.5%	31.9%	25.1%	19.2%
Puts	1.31	1.93	2.73	3.73	4.95	6.36	7.96	9.74	11.68
Deltas	19.4%	26.0%	33.5%	41.6%	49.8%	57.9%	72.3%	72.3%	78.2%
169.00 Calls	10.12	8.32	6.71	5.30	4.10	3.09	2.29	1.65	1.16
Deltas	77.4%	70.7%	63.1%	55.0%	46.7%	38.7%	31.1%	24.4%	18.6%
Puts	1.36	2.00	2.82	3.84	5.07	6.50	8.13	9.93	11.97
Deltas	20.0%	26.7%	34.3%	42.4%	50.6%	58.7%	66.2%	73.0%	78.8%
168.75 Calls	9.93	8.15	6.55	5.16	3.98	3.00	2.21	1.59	1.12
Deltas	76.8%	70.0%	62.3%	54.2%	45.9%	37.9%	30.4%	23.7%	18.0%
Puts	1.41	2.06	2.90	3.95	5.20	6.65	8.29	10.11	12.27
Deltas	20.6%	27.4%	35.0%	43.2%	51.5%	59.5%	67.0%	73.6%	79.9%
168.50 Calls	9.74	7.97	6.40	5.03	3.87	2.91	2.13	1.53	1.07
Deltas	76.2%	69.3%	61.5%	53.4%	45.1%	37.1%	29.7%	23.1%	17.5%
Puts	1.46	2.13	2.99	4.06	5.33	6.80	8.46	10.29	12.27
Deltas	21.2%	28.1%	35.8%	44.0%	52.3%	60.3%	67.7%	74.3%	79.9%

Date: 08.01.1988   British Pound 12/88

Chapter 4

Corporate Applications

What is the best hedge for my corporation: do nothing, use futures/forward contracts, buy options, sell options, range the risk or use a participating strategy? If the answer is options related what strike price(s) should I utilise?

The perfect solution can be graphed (for a hedger of a short Sterling position) as follows:

Figure 6

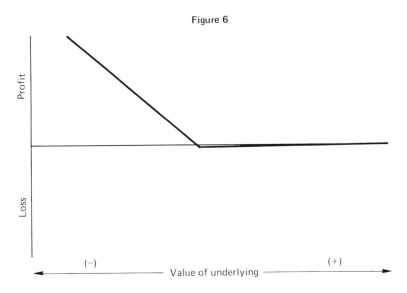

This graph is illustrative of an ATM call option on GBP but which is being offered in the market at a premium of zero. Thus if the value of the underlying currency rises the option provides full protection against losses. If the value of the underlying declines the option can be abandoned and the hedge undertaken in the foreign exchange markets. This theoretical option is the perfect hedge because it costs nothing to acquire. In the real world the nearest possible replication is the participating strategy. However the skill of hedging is to strike the delicate balance between risk, reward and expectation.

In order to compare the effects of strategies on a notional exchange risk position I have assumed a position of short (need to buy) £10 million for US Dollars 17 750 000 inter alia making the spot rate 1.7750. I have assumed a duration of 3 months and an outright forward rate which is 100 basis points lower than the current rate, i.e. 1.7650. The figures entitled Hedging Strategy Utilised show the effects of various hedges. I have started with a blank table and built a picture showing the estimated profit or loss which the hedge will provide over a range of values for the underlying currency at maturity of the transaction. The profit or loss is judged against a current spot exchange rate of 1.7750. See Figures 7, 8 and 9 (pages 37, 38 and 39).

Figure 7

HEDGING STRATEGY UTILISED

Do Nothing	Buy Futures		Buy Call OPTS	Write Put Options	Range the Risk (1)	Range the Risk (2)
Current Value						

Figure 8

HEDGING STRATEGY UTILISED

| | Do Nothing | Buy Futures | | Buy Call OPTS | Write Put Options | Range the Risk (1) | Range the Risk (2) |
		Actual	Opportunity	1.7750 Strike	1.7750 Strike	1.7500 to 1.8000	1.75 to 1.80 (PART)
1.8500							
1.8250							
1.8000							
Current Value 1.7750							
1.7500							
1.7250							
1.7000							

Figure 9

HEDGING STRATEGY UTILISED

	Do Nothing	Buy Futures/Fwd		Buy Call OPTS	Write put Options	Range the Risk (1)	Range the Risk (2)
		Actual	Opportunity	1.7750 Strike	1.7750 Strike	1.7500 to 1.8000	1.75 to 1.80 with 1.7250 Participation
1.8500	−750,000	+100,000	+850,000	−475,000	−225,000	−170,000	−250,000
1.8250	−500,000	+100,000	+600,000	−475,000	+25,000	−170,000	−250,000
1.8000	−250,000	+100,000	+350,000	−475,000	+275,000	−170,000	−250,000
Current Value 1.7750	NIL	+100,000	+100,000	−475,000	+525,000	+80,000	NIL
1.7500	+250,000	+100,000	−150,000	−225,000	+275,000	+330,000	+250,000
1.7250	+500,00	+100,000	−400,000	+25,000	+25,000	+330,000	+250,000
1.7000	+750,000	+100,000	−650,000	+275,000	−225,000	+330,000	+500,000

STRATEGY 1: DO NOTHING UNTIL MATURITY

This strategy assumes that the hedger takes no action until the US Dollar asset, Sterling liability, becomes current in June i.e. 3 months. It can be seen that the potential loss or gain is equal to the exact movements in the underlying and is unlimited. Graphically represented as follows:

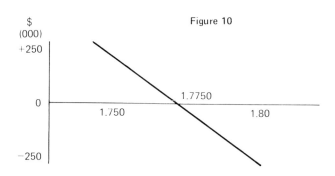

STRATEGY 2: PURCHASE JUNE EXPIRATION STERLING FORWARD FUTURES CONTRACTS NOW

This strategy assumes that the hedger covers the full exposure immediately by purchasing Sterling Forward Futures contracts in an amount of £10 million for June delivery. The basis differential (convergence) between the spot and futures price is US cents 1.00 and therefore the rate achieved is 1.7650.

By undertaking this strategy the hedger will achieve a saving of USD 100 000 over the current rate of 1.7650 (i.e. $1.00 × £10 m). These contracts purchased will protect the hedger against any rise in the value of Sterling between 'now' and the June futures date because the exchange rate is fixed at 1.7650. However, this strategy may give rise to an opportunity cost if the value of Sterling falls below 1.7650 between 'now' and the June futures date. This is illustrated by Figure 9 (page 39), the column entitled 'actual' shows savings versus today's rate of 1.7750, the column entitled 'opportunity' shows the potential opportunity cost (−) or opportunity saving (+) between the futures rate of 1.7650 and the various rates on maturity. Graphically this can be illustrated as follows:

Figure 11

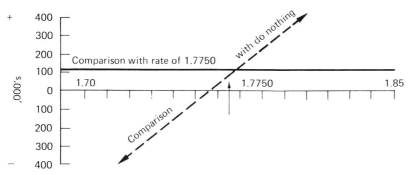

STRATEGY 3: PURCHASE JUNE EXPIRATION AT THE MONEY CALL OPTIONS ON STERLING

If the hedger purchased at the money call options on Sterling for June maturity he will be able to both ascertain the worst exchange rate which can be achieved and potentially benefit from any depreciation in the value of Sterling between 'now' and June. The cost of purchasing the option was US cents 4.75 and each pound of cover i.e. £10 m × $4.75 = USD 475 000. The hedger will have a simple choice at maturity:

Figure 12

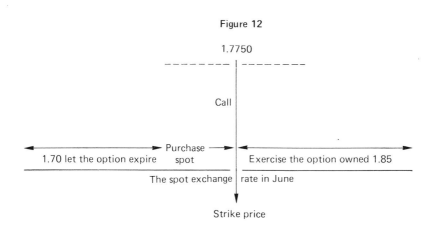

The attraction of purchasing options is that the position is 'insured', but in common with all insurance a fee is involved. However, there are few insurance policies which enable the holder to recoup more than the original premium without claiming against the policy. How can this be achieved using a Sterling call option to hedge this position? A fall in the value of Sterling will allow the hedger to abandon the option and purchase in the 'spot' market at maturity. This can best be illustrated by a comparison of doing nothing and purchasing futures.

It can be seen that by purchasing call options the worst excesses of loss are removed from the underlying position. There is also an added attraction that the hedger is not excluded from possible future savings.

This strategy is normally used when the hedger is expecting a substantial move in the value of the underlying position but is not sure in which direction the move will be. In the example a dramatic rise in the value of Sterling is protected at a cost of US $4.75 above the current exchange rate. If the value of Sterling falls the option can be abandoned and the conversion made at a rate more favourable than 1.7750, the normal breakeven rate on the downside is 1.7750 minus US $4.75.

You will find that options on most instruments afford a degree of protection which is greater than the usual market range. This also takes no account of the peace of mind, being hedged on both sides of the market argument.

STRATEGY 4: WRITE JUNE EXPIRATION AT THE MONEY PUT OPTIONS ON STERLING

I would not normally advocate the writing of options by other than professional traders, individuals and corporations who *really* understand the risk and who also have the cash resources to support the position if it does not turn out as planned. However, I would make one exception to this rule *provided* that the option writer:

(a) understands what he is doing and the possible likely outcomes, and,
(b) is prepared to be philosophical about the opportunity costs if they arise, and,
(c) can afford the necessary cash outflows if they occur, and,
(d) has a natural position or cash flows in the underlying instrument.

Why be so pessimistic about what is after all a fairly simple strategy? It is becaused covered option writing is often glossed over as a no/low risk strategy and therefore is not fully understood by many individuals and corporates outside of the investment community. This strategy will often provide an acceptable income stream for a substantial time but if the value of the underlying instrument moves dramatically the hedge cover is eroded or removed completely. To replace the hedge cover will often require substantially more options to be written than can be supported by the underlying cash flow position. This will become clearer if the graphical analysis is studied.

If the expectation is that the value of the Pound will not move during the life of the risk and this expectation proves to be correct, selling options against the cash flow is beneficial. The receipt of US cents 5.25 in premium will mitigate exchange loss to that extent either side of the current value of 1.7750.

If at maturity the value of the Pound is below 1.7750, the original rate which is also the strike price of the put which has been sold, the hedger will receive the premium of US cents 5.25. Therefore, compared to doing nothing the breakdown rate is 1.7225 (current value less the convergence of 0.0100), he is therefore 0.0425 better off i.e. the put premium of 0.0525 minus the convergence of 0.0100.

In summary if the spot rate at maturity of the risk is lower than at its inception the results are mixed depending where the rate settles. However, it is necessary to be philosophical because it can be seen that if the rate drops to 1.5750 an opportunity cost of USD 1 475 000 will have been incurred. If the hedger attempts to anticipate movements in the exchange rate and hedge against these after the puts have been sold, it may help or it may hinder the outcome but the original position has been changed beyond recognition.

If at maturity, or perhaps more correctly, during the life of the risk the rate starts to rise above 1.7750 the hedge cover begins to be eroded. At a rate of 1.8275 the hedge is completely exhausted and an open position reappears. This is the case because losses from 1.7750 to 1.8275 are covered by the premium of 0.0525 which has been received. There are two stages to look at this type of hedge, at maturity and during the life of the risk.

At maturity of the risk the situation is clear. Losses up to an exchange rate of 1.8275 are offset by the premium income (original rate 1.7750 plus premium of 0.0525), beyond this rate losses occur on a one for one basis with rises in the value of the pound. If no further action is taken losses above a rate of 1.8275 are real additional costs which must be added to the original. See Figures 13 and 14 (page 44).

Figure 13

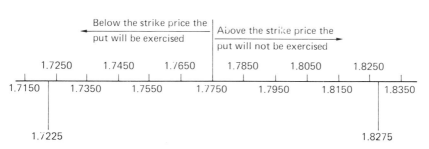

Figure 14

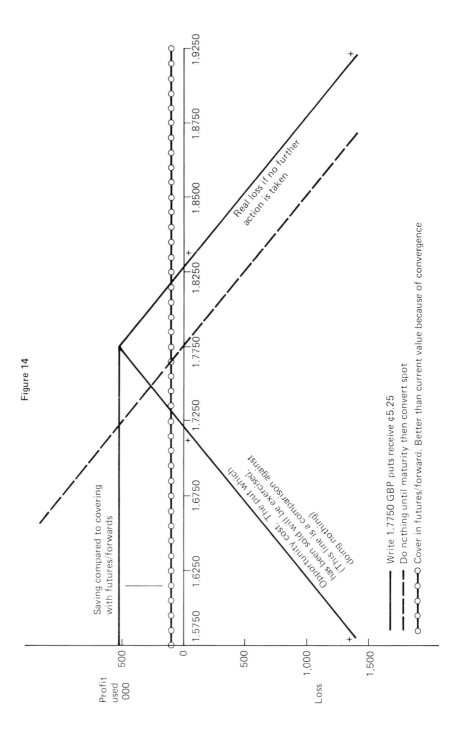

Write 1.7750 GBP puts receive ¢5.25
Do nothing until maturity then convert spot
Cover in futures/forward. Better than current value because of convergence

STRATEGY 5: RANGE THE RISK BETWEEN EXCHANGE RATES OF 1.75 AND 1.80

This strategy has been given a number of generic names by institutions offering this service. The name normally ascribed is cylinder option, but it is also called range forward, low/no cost option or budget hedge. The intention of the hedger is to ensure that the future exchange risk is held between two exchange rates. This end is achieved by simultaneously buying a call/put option and selling a put/call option.

In the example described, the hedger has an underlying requirement to purchase Pounds and therefore would need to undertake the following exercise:

(a) Purchase   1.80 calls on Sterling
(b) Sell   1.75 puts on Sterling.

It can be seen that this strategy can be undertaken for nil cost and indeed, frequently, the hedger will receive a payment for undertaking this transaction. The cost or income which arises is a function of the two option strike prices used to calculate the range.

The following table shows how, at maturity, exchange cover is provided to the hedger. It is inadvisable to enter into this strategy if it cannot be left until maturity because the hedger is left open to the vagaries of volatility. It should also be noted that if the underlying currency moves dramatically during the life of the strategy and American options are used, the hedger might be 'early exercised', therefore, it is arguably better to use European options where no danger of early exercise exists.

If at maturity the rate is lower than 1.75 the owner of the put which the hedger sold will provide Pounds at that rate.	Between the two rates in the band no option exercise takes place. Hedger fulfils the requirements in the spot market.	Protection at a rate of 1.80 or higher is provided by the 1.80 call which the hedger owns.
◀━━━━━━━━━━▶	◀━━━━━━━━━━▶	◀━━━━━━━━━━▶
PUT IS EXERCISED	BUY SPOT POUNDS	EXERCISE THE CALL

The value of the underlying currency at maturity.

1.70	1.75	1.80	1.85

It can be seen from this diagram that the hedger will fulfill his requirement for Sterling in one of three ways *but* at all times the worst rate (1.80) is known. In addition, the hedger may benefit down to a rate of 1.75.

It was previously stated that the cost or income derived from this strategy is a function of the exchange rates used. The exchange rates used are themselves a function of the expectations which the hedger has for the underlying currency. They are also a function of the amount of risk (between the current rate and the strike price of the option which is providing protection) that he is willing to bear.

There is one further enhancement which can be added to this strategy. That is to purchase a further out-of-the-money option to provide a pay back if the value of the underlying moves dramatically beyond the rate at which the hedger has sold the option.

This enhancement is particularly attractive in circumstances where the ordinary range the risk can be put on for a credit. The credit which would have been received could be used to purchase an out-of-the-money option and is a reasonably cheap method to benefit if a sharp movement in the underlying occurs.

The example I have in mind is when the Pound dropped to a rate of USD 1.05 and the hedger had to sell Pounds and purchase US Dollars. All of the potential hedges could conceivably have been expensive with the exception of two. Namely, this version of ranging the risk, and to do nothing. Conventional wisdom at the time dictated that there were no buyers of currencies and sellers of US Dollars except the Central Banks and it would have been a brave man who did nothing in those circumstances.

Chapter 5

Options from a Dealing Room Manager's Perspective

Options have certainly received their fair share of media coverage in the last five years. It is perhaps inevitable that only the 'bad news' stories receive high profile coverage and therefore it is perhaps also inevitable that many misconceptions exist about options.

Options are dangerous! Options are highly speculative! Options are expensive! etc. Is there any truth in these statements? Well the answer is Yes and No. There is an element of truth and much misplaced conjecture surrounding the subject.

The crucial and often misplaced distinction concerning the attendant risks of options are:

Options purchased = LIMITED RISK
Options sold = UNLIMITED RISK

If options purchased equate to white and options sold equate to black there are myriad shades of grey between the two extremes. The most important issue from a dealing room manager's perspective is a thorough understanding of the ultimate risk which his trader is running and a realistic 'game plan' to bring into play if the desire to continue running the risk changes. A properly thought-out strategy will provide for control of risk which is a crucial pre-requisite before any trading occurs.

To examine the issue of risk involved in currency options it is necessary to differentiate between options purchased and options written. This is possibly an over-simplification because strategies or combinations of options purchased and written may affect the degree of risk but, and this fact is true for any of the three categories, a valuation model will provide answers for an infinite number of questions regarding the risk. Interpreting the answers or information that the valuation model gives is critical in that strategies can be constructed to limit the degree of risk which the institution wishes to run. Degrees of risk will, of course, vary from institution to institution.

OPTIONS PURCHASED: LIMITED RISK

By its nature the option purchased provides the buyer with the right but not the obligation to conclude a foreign exchange transaction. For this right the purchaser pays a fee, this fee being the limit of his financial obligation and is inter alia the sum total of his risk involved. There is, of course, a counterparty credit risk issue which should be addressed. Consider the example of an option purchaser paying USD 50 000 for a three month option. Three points are important here, namely:

(1) The option purchaser has to pay (usually on day one) USD 50 000 in cash to another party in exchange for the rights contained in the option and therefore has a counterparty credit risk. This may be supported by a clearing house guarantee in the case of exchange traded options. This frequently turns the risk into a joint and several risk for all of the members of the exchange.
(2) The extent of the option purchaser's risk is limited to USD 50 000 but it is possible (although not highly probable) that the premium paid could be reduced substantially in a short space of time, e.g. the 'Dollar/Mark' exchange rate moved quite sharply from a rate of 1.75 to 1.65 in late 1987. A holder of an at the money (or in the money) unhedged Deutschemark put, US Dollar call option would have seen the value of his option reduced over a fairly short space of time. The moral here is that although the risk which the option purchaser bears is limited to the amount of the premium paid, it should be borne in mind that it is a risk nevertheless. If the option purchaser is not prepared to lose all of the premium paid, he, arguably, should not be entering into the position in the first place. It is advisable to utilise the valuation model to ensure that the premium paid fits the desired maximum potential loss which can be incurred and is also concurrent with the expectations of movements which prompted the original position to be entered into.
(3) The premium paid, if arrived at by reference to the expectation of movement in the underlying currency and its representative of an acceptable risk, will purchase (in this example) three months of time in which the expected events can occur.

To summarise, the risks attendant in options purchased strategies are acceptable if the three outlined points are considered before the transactions are concluded. If these 'rules of thumb' are borne in mind no option purchaser should be open to nasty surprises and can safely assess the risk reward ratio and satisfy himself of all eventualities before they occur. It is up to the reader to decide whether he believes that options purchased are 'dangerous, speculative, expensive, etc'.

OPTIONS SOLD: UNLIMITED RISK

Options sold present a much more complex and higher risk profile if they are left unhedged and can give rise to substantial losses if they are not properly controlled. The two most frequent causes of losses in positions which have been sold are the gradual changes in value and the sudden and unexpected event.

The gradual changes in value, irrespective of whether it is implied volatility, the value of the underlying currency, or interest rate differentials is possibly the most difficult to legislate against. To profit from options (in a trading environment) it is necessary to have a view and accept a degree of risk. If a short position is established to take advantage of a perceived occurrence and the perception is misplaced, at some stage the position has to be liquidated. Under these circumstances the temptation always exists to suggest that the unexpected event is only a 'technical correction, etc and the position will right itself in the end'. This may in fact prove to be the case but an institution would not enter into an unlimited loss strategy in any other instrument without first having defined the amount of risk it wished to bear and the amount of loss it is prepared to accept. It is usual to set a 'stop loss' against such a position. So should it be with short option positions, except perhaps the choice of how to 'stop out' a wrong position is easier because more choices exist. The three most obvious ways of 'stopping out' a losing position is to purchase the original position back, purchase some out of the money options to avoid further losses if the value of the underlying currency continues on its unexpected path, and purchase some options and enter into some futures positions to avoid further losses if volatility continues to rise contrary to expectations. (The combination of options and futures will neutralise the effect of movements in the underlying currency, the extent to which this should be undertaken can best be judged by reference to the valuation model). A word of caution—futures positions in isolation will not eliminate risk. In a market which is 'whip sawing', futures positions can unbalance the book and cause hedging losses, if they have to be liquidated at a later stage. It is not advisable to use futures positions to hedge a short option position on anything other than a short term basis and as a stop gap measure.

Just as it is impossible to insure a house as it is burning down, or a car as it is crashing, so too it is impossible to try to hedge a short option position after a sudden and unexpected event, unless of course, you are prepared to pay a greatly increased premium. Option history is littered with examples of losses caused by unexpected events which, although they happen very infrequently, give rise to the biggest losses. To cite but a few cases. In the mid 1980s the Deutsch Bundesbank was successful in intervening in the foreign exchange markets and in one trading session increased the value of the Deutschemark against the US Dollar from a rate of 3.43 to a rate of

3.27, a move of Pfenigs 16. Imagine the effect on the premium of an out of the money call on the Mark (at say 3.40) which had possibly been valued previously at Pfenigs 2 premium. Another example was 19 October, 1987 when the value of the Dow Jones Industrial Average fell 507 points (or somewhere approaching 20% of its value). Stock Index Put Options and put options on individual shares both in the US and in other major financial centres gained in value at a dramatic rate leaving any short position holder with substantial losses.

Complacency can often creep in because this type of unexpected event is the exception rather than the rule. Put options written in a rising market and call options written in a falling market will provide revenue for the writer of the option.

However, it is as well to recognise at the outset that these positions are far from riskless and indeed the risk reward ratio greatly favours the buyer of the option. If you are now beginning to believe that writing options is a 'no win' situation do not be put off. Option writing is as valid a strategy as option buying *so long as* the writer fully understands the risk that he is running and the risk is an acceptable one to the institution.

Parallels were drawn between insuring a car or house during an accident and hedging the risk in an unhedged short option portfolio after an unexpected event. The end result is the same in both instances. If the damage can be corrected, it will certainly prove to be a very costly exercise.

Although it was an unusual event it is worth examining what would have happened to a short DEM 3.40 call on the day that the Dollar/Mark fell from 3.43 to 3.27 and the call writer had Pfenigs 2.00 of premium left to his credit. Assume that the position was for just US 1 m and a 40% futures hedge at 3.43 was in place and assume that the futures hedge ratio moved from 40% to 90% during the course of the trading day.

Short DEM 3 400 000 call × delta 40% =

                              Delta Equiv Posn − DEM 1 360 000

Long DEM 1 360 000 futures × delta 100% =

                              Delta Equiv Posn + DEM 1 360 000

                   Net Delta Equiv Posn   NIL

Closing position:

Short DEM 3 400 000 call × delta 90% =

                              Delta Equiv Posn − DEM 3 060 000

Long DEM 1 360 000 futures × delta 100% =

                              Delta Equiv Posn + DEM 1 360 000

                   Net Delta Equiv Posn − DEM 1 700 000

End of day revaluation:

Short DEM 1 700 000 futures – option rate 3.40 = USD 500 000
reval rate   3.27 = USD 519 878

Loss = USD 19 878
Premium held DEM 20 000 @ 3.27   + USD   6 116

Net Loss − USD   13 762

It is also necessary to cover the additional 10% of the face value of the option at some time (the difference between the delta at 90% and the face value of 100% assuming that you are exercised). If this occurs at the same rate of 3.27 the cost will be an additional:

DEM 340 000 @ option rate   3.40 = USD 100 000
DEM 340 000 @ final purchase rate   3.27 = USD 103 975

− USD   3 975

The losses can be offset against the original futures hedge profit on DEM 1 360 000 which was owned at the beginning of the day at a rate of 3.43.

DEM 1 360 000 @ opening rate   3.43 = USD 396 501
DEM 1 360 000 @ option rate   3.40 = USD 400 000

Profit USD   3 499

This gives a final risk reward profile as follows:

Reward/Option

Option Premium   + USD 6 111
Futures Position profit   + USD 3 499

− USD 9 615

Risk/Loss
Delta adjustment loss on day   − USD 19 878
Final delta adjustment loss (10%)   − USD 3 975

− USD 23 853

Nett loss on strategy USD 14 238.

After a large sharp change in the value of any underlying commodity the markets usually become increasingly more volatile and this will give the option writer further problems to grapple with. If it is decided to continue to run the short option position and delta hedge until maturity, the likelihood of increased hedging losses will occur as markets move up and down more frequently. If it is decided that the original position should be re-purchased, the premium cost necessary to achieve this will reflect not only the 'exchange loss' but, in all probability, a much higher implied volatility element as option writers temporarily become scarcer.

In summary of the risks involved in selling options, it is suggested that an *uncontrolled* position can be risky, but a well thought out and hedged short position need not be so. By reference to the valuation model, strategies can be as risky or risk free as the seller desires. It is up to the seller to decide the likelihood of a major move. Large moves are obviously not an every day occurrence but if they happen, are the consequences acceptable?

Most trading rooms employ traders to trade in spot currencies and of course they expect the individuals to do so profitably. If, for example, a trader is continuously trading a particular currency and therefore managing the institution's risk in that currency, why not give him the advantage of being paid by a third party for managing the same risk? In other words, if he can trade spot 'cable' successfully, starting each day with a nil profit position, why not give him the advantage of some option premiums (from options written) to assist him further with his task. Don't be tempted! Spot trading and options management are two entirely different disciplines. Spot trading is a short term, high turnover situation with the trader having the ability to change his mind on the direction of the underlying as frequently as is necessary. Option trading requires a longer term perspective and reference to other criteria than just the value of the underlying.

Hopefully, the myths of options being 'dangerous, etc' have now been dispelled. If the risks are properly controlled, options trading can be an additional profitable entity within a dealing room. Examples of the ways in which options can be combined to achieve various risk reward scenarios are shown in Chapter 6, Trading Strategies.

The following are some of the practical issues which will need to be addressed before trading can commence.

Prior to commencing dealing in currency options, it is necessary to give careful consideration to the objectives of the bank for wanting to be involved with this particular instrument. Is the motivation position taken for profit, hedging of bank positions, customer service or market making? Each of these different motivations requires a different approach. However, there are a number of requirements which will be needed for all four fields. They are as follows:

(1) A thorough understanding of the instrument by at least one trader and the department head.

(2) An option valuation model. This can either be a simple programmable calculator type or a propriety system, depending on the degree of involvement.
(3) A clear understanding of the type of risks the bank wishes to assume. This can be defined in a policy manual, such a document helping to crystallise thoughts.

Further consideration needs to be given to counterparty credit risk, a subject which is somewhat simplified if just using listed markets. However even then there are matters of credit which need to be addressed in relation to the broker and margin arrangements.

To start by discussing the items which should be covered by the policy manual.

Currencies

Is the object of the exercise to write options based on historical volatility and delta hedge using the spot markets? It is possible to write options in almost any major convertible currency. This is not a good first step. It is advisable to quote options only where there is a market in options together with a spot currency market. The reason for this is that if your prediction of future volatility proves to be badly wrong and you wish to close out your short option position, it is not possible. Therefore, you have to carry the risk to maturity which in certain circumstances can be disastrous viz South African Rand. In addition, the current modus operandi in the foreign exchange markets is for most currencies to react (at least to some extent) in parallel against the US Dollar. Therefore, if you are using futures to delta hedge, say, Cable DEM, CHF, and Yen, it is impossible to monitor and trade all four positions simultaneously without missing at least part of a move.

If buying and selling the same option (usually to cover a client's requirement) then the only risk is that of counterparty, the currency is not relevant so long as the 'nostros', general ledgers and the option accounting model are properly set up for recording and accounting of transactions.

Periods forward to deal (maturity)

There has been much discussion about the relative merits of the 'OTC' versus the listed markets. Both have advantages and disadvantages and these are relevant to the question of the maturity of deals. Taking first the 'OTC' market, it is usually possible to get a price up to one year in the major currencies, however, the prices in the longer periods may be scarce at the time and will almost certainly be fairly wide. The majority of deals in the 'OTC' market take place between one month and six months—it is unusual to find options of a shorter duration than one month readily available other than on the listed markets.

In the listed markets the maturity schedule is different to that of the OTC market with most exchanges quoting quarter dates, usually mid March, June, September and December. In addition, at the time of writing some exchanges quote two further months which allow for that exchange always to have a quote available in its currencies in the first three calendar months. The best liquidity usually exists in the first four contracts, although it is of course quite possible to deal in the back month contracts, but the prices again may tend to be wide. Initially at least, it is worth establishing parameters, of, say, six months for 75% of the book and up to twelve months for 25% for the major currencies (i.e. GBP, DEM, CHF, JPY) and then adjust percentages and maturity to suit your own experience. It is worth noting that options with maturities of less than one month will not be the easiest to hedge in volatile markets. For this reason it is prudent to avoid being short of too many 'short dated' options. Being long on short dated options is less of a problem because the maximum loss is known at the outset and if the object of being long on 'short dated' options is to delta hedge this can be done profitably in volatile markets.

Which markets to utilise

The choice of which market or markets to use is growing rapidly as more and more exchanges offer currency option products. It is advisable to choose one listed market per time zone and the 'OTC' market on which to commence trading. If it is so desired, there is no reason why one should not have open positions on all the exchanges, but they each have their own idiosyncracies which could mean that the option you have granted is slightly superior to the one you have purchased and this could leave you open to losses. In addition, option margins tend to be expensive and although you may be 'long' on one exchange and 'short' on another in the same contract it may be necessary to support both positions with margins which may not earn interest. The same arguments apply when choosing a clearing agent. It is best to find one that provides services to as many exchanges as possible. The question of splitting broking and clearing services is one of personal preference as is the question of direct access to the floor broker. The job of the broker/clearer in the listed markets is different to that of an 'OTC' broker in that the broker/clearer becomes part of the transaction and is the link between the bank and the clearing house (i.e. ICCH, IOCC, or OCC) and actually takes part in the process of exercise of the option and the subsequent transfer of funds and also the process of margining the open positions. The 'OTC' broker simply brings together two principals – one as buyer the other as seller – and receives a brokerage, the OTC broker has no further interest in the transaction. For these reasons it is worth establishing exactly what degree of risk you are prepared to accept on, firstly, your listed market broker, secondly, your listed market clearer (if you split broking and clearing), thirdly, the clearing house and fourthly, the OTC broker. You should also check to what extent the clearing house guarantee on listed markets covers your risks.

Appropriate size limits

Treasury Managers are conversant with the day to day management (or elimination) of foreign exchange or interest rate risk and will understand that if they give a spot dealer a one million Pound open limit, he will make or lose on 'Cable', for instance US \$10 000 per one cent movement. Similarly, if a deposit dealer loses two per cent pa on an overnight US \$ 10 000 000 he is down USD 555. (These are quantifiable risks and at the end of each day the Treasury Manager receives his P + L Summary and open position sheet which tells him how much his department has made or lost, or stands to make or lose overnight.)

With options, one is faced with the interactions of a number of factors which when combined, give a 'good estimate' of overnight exposure and potential profit and loss. In all but the most simple portfolio, I believe that it is essential to enlist the services of a good computer model to provide exposure reporting and profit and loss analysis. Listed below are all the factors which when added together make up an options 'price' and hedge ratio.

```
Strike Price
Current Spot
Current Domestic Interest Rate ) to calculate the forward rate
Current Foreign Interest Rate   )
Premium Interest Rate           ) to calculate interest to maturity
Number of Days to Maturity
Current Volatility
Whether a 'Put' or 'Call'
Whether 'European' or 'American' style
```

As will be quickly realised, if the value of the underlying currency volatility and time move, which invariably they will from one day to the next, it will be futile to try and estimate the overall effect on the option 'price' and its hedge ratio. It must be recalculated using up to date information. By segregating the various risk factors and applying limits to them, it is possible to provide for a comprehensive policy to cover most occurrences. The risk factors can be sub-divided as follows:

Delta Limits
Gamma Limit/Maximum Daily P + L Limit
Volatility Change Limit
Premium Paid Limit

The delta limit

The delta limit is a measure of the exposure to movement in the value of the underlying currency and the risk attached to a short position cannot be reduced by buying or selling the underlying currency. The reason for this is that you will only rebalance the book if the direction of movement is one way. If the movement is whipsaw, then by buying or selling the underlying currency you will set up an exposure opposite to that which you were trying to eradicate. For example:

A. Underlying at 1.80

Option/Cash Position	Delta %	Delta Equivalent Posn
− £1 mio Call 1.80	50	− £500 000
− £1 mio Put 1.80	50	+ £500 000

B. Underlying moves to 1.85

Option/Cash Position	Delta %	Delta Equivalent Posn
− £1 mio Call	75	− £750 000
− £1 mio Put	25	+ £250 000
		− £500 000
Purchase £$\frac{1}{2}$ mio Cash	100	+ £500 000

C. Underlying moves back to 1.80

− £1 mio Call	50	− £500 000
− £1 mio Put	50	+ £500 000
Long £$\frac{1}{2}$ mio Cash	100	+ £500 000
		+ £500 000

This example is very simplified and shows what would happen if spot moved from 1.80 to 1.85 and then back to 1.80 and the effect of the delta equivalent position if you just use futures or cash to hedge. In A you are square in delta equivalent terms at the current level of spot. When spot moves up to 1.85 in B you purchase £500 000 to hedge back to square. When spot moves back to 1.80 in C, your cash purchased at 1.85 is still in the book and you are therefore long in delta equivalent terms and need to dispose of the cash holding to regain your square position.

The delta limit need only apply to negative delta positions because a positive delta position means that any hedges undertaken in the spot at futures market will generate a profit and not a loss. However, there is a risk in being delta positive (or perhaps more properly termed gamma positive), but the risk management of this position is covered in the gamma/maximum daily P + L limit.

The size of the delta limit applied to the book (assuming that you are trading either for gain or as a market maker) will vary from bank to bank but should at least in part be a reflection of the size of spot positions normally taken. Do not set a delta limit in the options book of USD 10 mio if you normally take spot positions of USD 2 mio. The risks are broadly similar with the losses in options only mitigated to the extent of the daily time value received.

If you are using an option to establish a foreign exchange position which is intended to be either a short or medium term strategic position, you can to all intents ignore the delta position and look at the premium you will have to write off if your assumptions are wrong about the underlying currency. There are two provisos; firstly, do not establish short options positions for strategic purposes. If you are convinced enough to take the position out initially, you should be prepared to pay a premium not to get stopped out if in the short term the underlying currency moves in the opposite direction to that which you expected. Secondly, does your supervisory authority require you to count options purchased as part of your 'spot' limit and therefore if you purchase an option, will you be within your delegated limits? If it is decided to take a three month view on a currency and purchase a strategic option position, this should probably be done away from the spot trading desk. Psychologically, it is difficult for the spot trader to be short if he knows that his manager is long.

You will find that the judicious use of strategies to establish strategic positions will give more consistent results than just buying or selling of options. Option strategies are covered in Chapter 6. You are not limited to the twenty strategies I have listed.

Mark to market on a regular basis

By marking to market on a regular basis, preferably daily, you will know at all times your current profit or loss on the open position and can take steps to realise it. The disadvantage of using this method for medium term strategic positions is that you will be taking unrealised losses and profits to account. It is prudent to do so with losses because that is the realisable value of the position if you decide to terminate at that time. In the case of strategic positions it is more difficult to assess the value of taking unrealised gains to P + L because if the value of the underlying currency turns round, not only do you have potentially the cost of the option to write off, but also the unrealised gain which has been accounted for but may not now exist.

Account at the lower of cost or realisable

This is probably the most cautious method of accounting for strategic positions because you are writing off the cost of purchasing the option on a straight line basis over its life unless the current realisable value falls below the written off value. If this happens, an additional write off would be made to bring the written off value back into line with the current market value. There are possibly two problems with this method of valuation. It is important to be aware of how much profit (if any) you have over and above the written off value of the option and take steps to realise this profit at the appropriate time, either by selling the option or taking out a foreign exchange or other hedge. The second problem is that of carrying an asset in the books at less than its current realisable value. On balance it is believed that this method of accounting and valuing strategic positions is prudent. Agree this with your auditors, since they may argue that over quarter or year ends the position should be valued at the market price and additional profit be accounted for.

The gamma limit/maximum P + L limit

The gamma limit will show how exposed to potential profits and losses you are given changes in the level of the underlying currency. It will also provide a good measure of how overbought or oversold you are in option/delta terms. In the delta limit example it was demonstrated what happened if you hedged a position using the foreign exchange market. The following example shows what happens if you hedge the same position using another option although not necessarily for the same strike price or maturity.

A. Underlying at 1.80

Option	Strike	Delta %	Delta Equiv Posn.
− £1 mio Call	1.80	50%	− £500 000
+ £1 mio Call	1.81	45%	+ £450 000
			− £ 50 000

B. Underlying moves to 1.85

− £1 mio Call	1.80	85%	− £850 000
+ £1 mio Call	1.81	78%	+ £780 000
			− £ 70 000
Purchase £70 000 cash		100%	+ 70 000

C. Underlying moves back to 1.80

− £1 mio Call	1.80	50%	− £500 000
+ £1 mio Call	1.81	45%	+ £450 000
Long £70 000		100%	+ £ 70 000
			+ £ 20 000

It can be seen from this example that there is still exposure to movements in spot but they are of a much more manageable size and by setting a realistic gamma limit you will remove the requirements to continually rehedge substantial amounts in the foreign exchange markets. You do, however, need to take into consideration the fact that because you are purchasing different options you will have a different cost and should take into consideration the maximum loss which can be achieved, firstly, on a daily basis and secondly, until maturity of the portfolio.

The maximum daily profit and loss can be gauged by using an options valuation model. If a portfolio is traded, it should be on a mark to market basis. Decisions can then be taken on a current value basis. It is necessary to do 'what if' scenarios to ascertain the effect of either buying or selling options to rehedge the position.

It is impossible to go into every conceivable scenario here, but assuming that you have a model and are trading a portfolio of options for gain, you should be able to do 'what if' scenarios before you enter into a position. Also, by undertaking this exercise you will be able to gauge what your potential exposure to losses is overnight and take corrective action if necessary. A common sense approach to option profit and loss pays dividends as can be seen from the example of an end of day position which shows what will happen from today until tomorrow over a range of spot positions.

		Delta Equiv Posn	*Overnight P + L*
	1.82	− £1 000 000	− USD 17 000
	1.81	− £ 500 000	− USD 2 000
Current spot	1.80		+ USD 3 000
	1.79	+ £ 500 000	− USD 2 000
	1.78	+ £1 000 000	− USD 17 000

The figures used are for illustrative purposes and are therefore simplified, but the story that they tell is of a portfolio which is short on options and will need rehedging if spot moves overnight. The overnight P + L column shows the effective profits and losses if no hedges are undertaken until the value of the underlying is at the spot level in the first column. At the current spot level, the profit of USD 3 000 is earned because of time decay in the options sold. The losses arise because you will have to purchase or sell foreign exchange after the move has occurred. Do not forget that you cannot anticipate a spot movement and purchase or sell foreign exchange in anticipation and still remain hedged because you will simply unbalance the position. For example if you think Sterling is going up overnight and you purchase GBP 500 000 to hedge, this is what happens.

	Delta Equiv Posn	*Overnight P + L*
1.82	+ £ 500 000	− USD 7 000
1.81		+ USD 3 000
Current spot 1.80	+ £ 500 000	+ USD 3 000
1.79	+ £1 000 000	− USD 7 000
1.78	+ £1 500 000	− USD 27 000

A better way to rehedge against an expected rise in the value of Sterling overnight is to purchase some call options. This picture then changes as follows:

	Delta Equiv Posn	*Overnight P + L*
1.82	+ £200 000	− USD 3 000
1.81	£100 000	+ USD 500
Current spot 1.80		+ USD 1 500
1.79	+ £100 000	− USD 500
1.78	+ £200 000	− USD 3 000

The extent of the delta equivalent position and the overnight P + L will depend on what options are purchased. The figures used are for illustrative purposes only.

The degree of sophistication in measuring exposure can be increased as you get more proficient in using options, but initially the daily P + L is an excellent starting point and common sense will prevail. If you are unhappy with the exposure to losses, you can take steps to avoid them. It is also important to look beyond the potential P + L from today until tomorrow and the effect on the portfolio of movements in time. This can be achieved by doing 'what if' scenarios on the model.

Volatility change limit

The volatility change limit should be self explanatory. The implied volatility used in the models to calculate P + L should be updated regularly. This exercise will have the effect of giving you extra profit if you are long volatility and the implied volatility rises, or giving you losses if you are long volatility and the implied volatility falls. Conversely, if you are short volatility and the implied volatility rises, you will incur losses. If it falls you will receive profits.

To calculate the effect of rises or falls in implied volatility, a matrix is produced by your model. To simplify this example, assume that the implied volatility is the same for all periods. This is not the case and implied volatility for monthly periods should be used. The following example assumes that current US Dollar versus Sterling implied volatility is constant at 10% for all periods. What are the effects over a range of prices in, firstly, a long book and secondly, a short book?

Long Book in Volatility

	12%	+ USD 40 000
	11%	+ USD 20 000
Current Volatility	10%	−/ Nil
	9%	− USD 20 000
	8%	− USD 40 000

Short Book in Volatility

	12%	− USD 40 000
	11%	− USD 20 000
Current Volatility	10%	−/ Nil
	9%	+ USD 20 000
	8%	+ USD 40 000

The figures used here are purely for illustrative purposes and will depend on the size and maturity profile of the portfolio and the changes in implied volatility for the various periods.

Implied volatility is a supply and demand market and will reflect expectations of movements in the value of the underlying currency and forthcoming news and economic data.

The profits and losses produced as a result of changes in volatility are not additional to your trading book and need not be booked separately. They do, however, exist and will be incurred in your trading book when you update the implied volatility. It is therefore important to be aware what will happen to your profit and loss position in your trading book when you re-adjust the level of implied volatility.

The simplest method of setting a volatility change limit is by numerical sum. For example (again this will be a reflection on the size of the book and the bank) for every volatility change of 1% it is only acceptable to endure a USD 10 000 loss. Alternatively, you could say that whatever happens to implied volatility the loss cannot exceed, say, USD 50 000. Implied volatility tends not to increase by 5% overnight but it can move up quite quickly when central bank intervention happens and the market and the central banks are at odds about the correct level of the underlying currency.

Premium paid limit

The premium paid limit can be used as a further gauge as to how overbought or oversold in options your institution currently is. This limit is easily monitored because when you start to trade in options you will need to open this account in the General Ledger. The limit will quite simply be a measure of the outstanding balance on this account, and will highlight the following potential dangers.

Premium paid

If your trader decides that markets are going to become more volatile and he purchases options to take advantage of this situation, he will have a negative daily carry because of erosion of time value. Alternatively, he may decide that the value of the underlying currency is moving in a particular direction and may purchase currency options to take advantage of this situation. Similarly, he would be subject to a negative daily carry because of erosion of time value, or worse, if the value of the underlying moves in the opposite direction to expectation, the options purchased could lose value. The premium paid limit will ensure that your losses are known and are at an acceptable level to your institution.

Premium received

If your premium paid account is showing a substantial credit balance, it means that you are in essence short of options and therefore are subject to changes in implied volatility and movements in the value of the underlying currency. If your credit balance is substantial, it does not give you a direct view of the risks involved but it is a simple 'alert signal' to look at the structure of the book.

Other potential exposure inherent in the portfolio

There is an additional risk in running an option portfolio. That is the risk of movements in the two relative interest rates as defined by the forward swap.

This risk is accentuated when writing American call options on a high interest rate currency and then purchasing the underlying currency and purchasing an American put option in cover (technically called a conversion).

Sterling versus US Dollars

Write Sterling call with strike of say 1.80 on GBP 1 mio received cent 2.0
Purchase GBP 1 mio spot at 1.80
Purchase GBP 1 mio put with strike 1.80 cost cent 2.60
Swap DBP 1 mio 1 month forward receive cent 0.60 for swap.

At first inspection you have a locked in arbitrage at maturity of the strategy because:

(a) If Sterling rises in value, the call and the cash move on a one for one basis therefore when the call is exercised you have the cash to fulfill your obligations.
(b) If Sterling falls in value, the cash and the put move on a one for one basis and when the call expires worthless you would apply the cash against the put which you own.

In this example the premium paid for the put purchased is equal to the income received for writing the call PLUS the forward swap point gained for buying forward Sterling. This is called put call parity and is a measure that the market is trading at the correct level. However, there is a forward swap-foreign exchange risk inherent in this transaction and that is the risk of early exercise as a result of a rise in the value of the underlying currency.

Consider the two following examples:

I No Early Exercise

Write Call 1.80	Sterling rises,) At
	call is exercised) maturity
Own Cash 1.80	
Buy Put 1.80	Sterling falls,) of
	you exercise) strategy
	put

Write Call received	cents	2.00
Buy Put pay	cents	2.60
Forward swap income	cents	0.60

NIL

II Early Exercise Takes Place

Write Call 1.80			Sterling rises, call is exercised prior to maturity
Own Cash 1.80			
Buy Put 1.80			
Write call received	cents	2.00 +	
Buy Put pay	cents	2.60 −	
Forward swap income	cents	0.60 +	(original swap points)
Forward swap cost	cents	0.30 −	(cost of reversing swap)
TOTAL COST	CENTS	0.30 −	

The forward swap cost is incurred because originally you anticipated a swap income of cents 0.60 (say for one month period) but were actually exercised after say 15 days and had to reverse the swap to fulfill your obligations under the option contract. This scenario would only occur if the option delta on the call had moved to 100% as a result of the rise in the value of Sterling. There is an additional cost in this transaction, the finance of the exchange loss from new swap date until the maturity of the existing swap. This occurs because all swaps in the foreign exchange market must be undertaken at current exchange rates. Current exchange rates will be higher than exchange rates on the original swap or early exercise would not have taken place. It is necessary to finance the cash difference at an interest cost.

Forward risk arises in an option portfolio which contains American options because of the above situation and also because the date of exercise of each position is not known with any degree of certainty at the outset. The problem which arises is:

> To cover forward and risk having to re-adjust, or to swap day to day and risk changes in the forward rates which will mean forward cost or income will be greater or less than originally expected?

An absolute answer is not immediately obvious. If cash is being used to hedge a portfolio a compromise mix of forward and day to day swaps is often used. If futures are being used the problem is to some extent mitigated, but the spot/futures convergence will still change in line with changes in interest rate differentials.

In the introduction to this book it was suggested that currency option trading is 75% science and 25% art. The art of trading cannot be learned from books, it can only be learned by working with a computer model. The model will give mathematical answers to mathematical questions and is just a tool to make control and decision making simpler; it cannot replace the value judgements of the trader who has a 'feel' for the market. If the valuation model tells you that you have a potential loss of, say, USD 50 000 if the value of the underlying moves 2% overnight, and if it also tells you that you will receive, say, USD 5 000 of income if the value of the underlying does not move overnight, the choice of what, if any, decision to take is yours. Do not blame the messenger if he does not tell you what you want to hear, the choices are all yours.

It has become popular to use letters of the Greek alphabet when discussing option theory. The generally ascribed values are as follows (for which I am indebted to Sheldon Natenberg, President of Professional Options Consultants, Chicago):

Delta

1. The ratio of option contracts to underlying contracts required to establish a neutral hedge.
2. The number of underlying contracts which the owner of a call is long, or which the owner of a put is short.
3. The rate of change of the theoretical value of an option with respect to its underlying.
4. The probability that the option will finish in-the-money.

Each of the above definitions of delta is, essentially, the same.

Gamma

The rate of change of an option's delta for 100 basis points move in the underlying example: If an option has a delta of .35 and a gamma of .05, then the option can be expected to have a delta of .40 if the underlying goes up one point, and a delta of .30 if the underlying goes down one point. The gamma is often referred to as the option's *curvature*.

It may be helpful to think of the delta as the 'speed' with which an option moves with respect to its underlying. The maximum 'speed' is 100% for very deeply in-the-money options, and the minimum 'speed' is zero for the very far out-of-the-money options. Continuing with this analogy, the gamma would be the 'acceleration' of the option, i.e. how fast it picks up or loses 'speed' (deltas) as the underlying advances or declines.

Theta

An option's loss in theoretical value for each day that the underlying sits still. Example: An option with a theta of .005 will lose approximately half of one tick in theoretical value for each day that the underlying fails to move. The theta of an option is more commonly referred to as its *time decay*.

Vega (also known as kappa)

The sensitivity of an option's theoretical value to a change in volatility. Example: An option with a vega of .15 would gain (lose) 15 ticks in theoretical value for each percentage point increase (decrease) in the volatility estimate.

Rho

The sensitivity of an option's theoretical value to a change in interest rates. Options on futures contracts are relatively insensitive to changes in interest rate.

Lambda

The leverage or gearing of an option.

It is not being suggested that limits should not be set for all of the aforementioned risk factors. Equally, the wisest course to take when beginning to trade a book of options might be to start small and gradually build up book size and complexity as confidence and understanding grow. A case can be made to start with Chicago Mercantile Exchange currency options. CME options are a liquid market which is important. There are two additional advantages with this market, namely that the contract size is small enough to allow fine tuning even for a modest book and at close spreads. In addition, there is a highly liquid futures market available in the underlying currency with matching dates to those of the option. This will facilitate ease of hedging and rehedging the book.

If trading is commenced in this manner you will find that you will wish to set your own limits to suit your own requirements and so long as they are set in a meaningful manner they will become helpful tools.

Almost all of the profit and loss profile graphs which are seen relate to currency options describing the maximum profit or loss to the writer/buyer at *expiration* of the position. Whilst this is helpful information to have, it is more relevant to the option buyer than the option writer. Option writers who only look at their position at the onset of strategy and at maturity will soon be ex-option writers. What is required is constant monitoring of risk and fine tuning of the book as circumstances change.

In summary, option management is similar to learning to drive a car. Books can be written describing how to drive a car, but it is doubtful if many people could read one and then get into a car and immediately drive perfectly. Most will learn the basics, then get into the car and learn through practice until, after a short period of time, they become competent. Even when you are competent there are things which it is unwise to attempt – 80 mph in a country lane. So too with option management, you are the best judge of your own competence and the wisdom of particular risks under particular circumstances. Assess the risk impartially. If the odds are 1000 to 1 against something happening, do you and your institution want to bear the effects of the one chance occurring?

Chapter 6

Trading Strategies

This chapter contains illustrations of the most popular and frequently used option strategies. Attempts are not made to describe every strategy which is used and, indeed, it is quite possible to construct strategies to meet requirements for particular circumstances. This chapter tries to illustrate strategies to an individual who is new to the subject of options, and to explain what effects will be achieved when particular strategies are undertaken.

Particular attention has been paid to the original cost or income of the strategy when it was initiated and the profit or loss at maturity. The 'one day' effect has been used to show the profit and loss profiles from today until tomorrow assuming no rehedging takes place in the interim period. Most options are of a 'traded' nature, and they will have a 'time value' through most of their life. To ascertain the value of an option prior to its maturity it is necessary to utilise a pricing model, or, if the option is 'exchange traded', the value can be ascertained by reference to the current trading prices. For the purpose of these illustrations, the dealing spreads and interim revaluations of positions have been ignored. Assume that no 'delta hedging' is undertaken, this subject is fully covered in the chapter on portfolio analysis. Also assume that any option which is out of the money at maturity will not be exercised and that any option which is in the money (even though it may only be so by a tiny amount) will be exercised. A nominal position of GBP 100,000 which represents 4 nominal futures positions of £25,000 each has been used.

It is possible to construct positions using other options and the underlying currency which will have the same properties as a particular strategy but may be marginally more efficient to purchase or sell. These positions are known as 'synthetics' and where it is appropriate, there is a description of the synthetic position relevant to the particular strategy.

I am indebted to the Chicago Mercantile Exchange for allowing me access to their option pricing models.

TYPE OF STRATEGY: Long Call Option

When to use

If you believe that the market will rise at some stage. If you believe that a rise is imminent buy a shorter option, e.g. one or two months. If you are unsure of the timing buy a longer option, e.g. six to nine months. In the case of the shorter option the leverage is greater but obviously the timing is more critical. In the case of the longer option the leverage is lower and the cost of the option higher but the 'time' purchased is much greater and therefore timing is less critical.

How to construct

1. Purchase a call in the market.
2. Purchase the underlying currency and purchase a put at the same time and with the same strike price as the current spot or forward rate.

The effects

1. If you are correct in your assumptions and the value of the underlying currency does appreciate –

   (a) The call will appreciate in value and can either be sold prior to maturity to recoup any residual time value or held until maturity and exercised.
   (b) The currency purchased will appreciate in value whilst the put purchased will gradually decrease in value but only to the extent of the original premium paid to purchase the option. The currency can be sold at any time in the spot market to realise the profit. The put can either be retained if a reversal is expected, or sold at the same time as the underlying currency.

2. If you are incorrect in your assumptions and the value of the underlying currency depreciates –

   (a) The call will decrease in value but only to the extent of the original premium paid to purchase the option.
   (b) The currency purchased will depreciate in value whilst the put purchased will increase in value, once the put goes in the money the maximum difference between the appreciation of the put and the depreciation of the underlying cannot exceed the original premium paid. The currency held can be sold at any time or delivered against

the put at maturity. If the currency is sold it is advisable to sell the put at the same time to realise the option profit which will offset the underlying currency loss.

Profit and loss characteristics

1. Losses are limited to the original premium paid to purchase the options.
2. Profits are unlimited and equate to Strike and Premium – underlying.

See Figures 15 and 16 (pages 71 and 72).

TYPE OF STRATEGY: Long Put Option

When to use

If you believe that the market will decline at some stage. If you believe that the decline is imminent buy a shorter option e.g. one or two months, if you are unsure of the timing buy a longer option e.g. six to nine months. In the case of the shorter option the leverage is greater but obviously the timing is more critical. In the case of the longer option the leverage is lower and the cost of the option higher but the 'time' purchased is much greater and therefore timing is less critical.

How to construct

1. Purchase a put in the market.
2. Sell the underlying currency and purchase a call option at the same time and with the same strike price as the current spot or forward rate.

The effects

1. If you are correct in your assumptions and the value of the underlying currency declines –

   (a) The put will increase in value and can either be sold prior to maturity to recoup any residual time value or held until maturity and exercised.
   (b) The short position in the underlying currency becomes cheaper to repurchase whilst the call purchased will gradually decrease in value but only to the extent of the original premium paid to purchase the option. The underlying currency can be repurchased at any time in

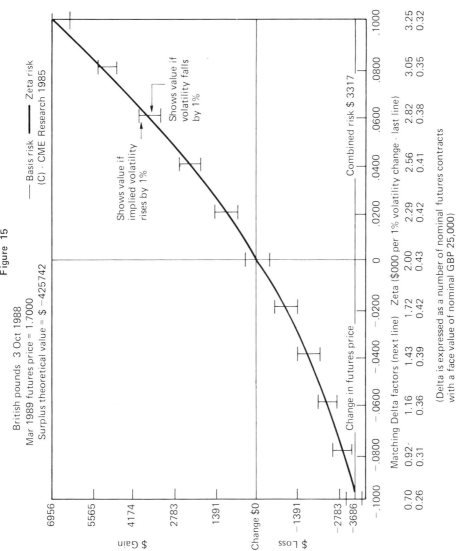

Figure 15

British pounds 3 Oct 1988
Mar 1989 futures price = 1.7000
Surplus theoretical value = $ −425742

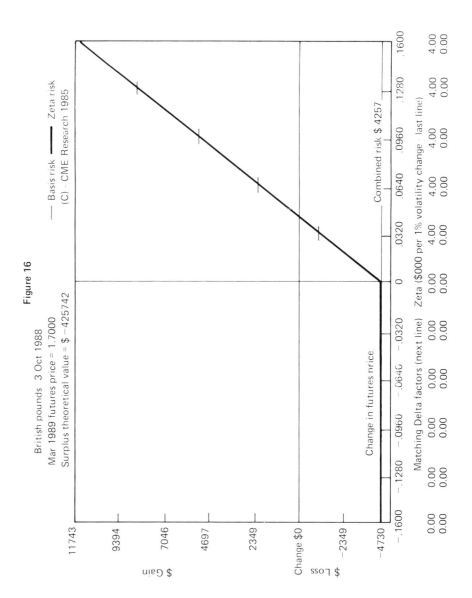

Figure 16

British pounds   3 Oct 1988
Mar 1989 futures price = 1.7000
Surplus theoretical value = $ -425742

Basis risk ——— Zeta risk
(C) · CME Research 1985

Combined risk $ 4257

Change in futures price

Zeta ($000 per 1% volatility change last line)
Matching Delta factors (next line)

the spot market to realise the profit. The call can either be retained if a reversal in the value of the underlying currency is expected, or sold at the same time as the underlying currency.

2. If you are incorrect in your assumptions and the value of the underlying currency appreciates –

   (a) The put will decrease in value but only to the extent of the original premium paid to purchase the option.
   (b) The short position in the underlying currency will start to show a loss whilst the long call option will show a profit to offset this position. The maximum loss which can be realised is the cost of the call option. At maturity the option will be exercised and the proceeds received will be utilised to close out the short position in the underlying currency. Alternatively, the option may be sold and the short position repurchased at the same time.

Profit and loss characteristics

1. Losses are limited to the original premium paid to purchase the option.
2. Profits are unlimited and equate to Strike and Premium – underlying.

See Figures 17 and 18 (pages 74 and 75).

TYPE OF STRATEGY: Short Call Option

When to use

If you believe that the market will stagnate or fall in value and are prepared to take an unlimited risk for a limited reward i.e. the premium received. The shorter the option period obviously the shorter the risk but the higher the 'gammas' which can cause problems if the seller is delta hedging (see Chapter 8). Care should also be taken when writing options of a longer duration (unless the strategy is against income streams). It is quite possible to bear the risk for say five months of a six month option successfully and in the final month see a sharp move in the value of the underlying currency which will remove all the profit previously earned and create a loss before maturity.

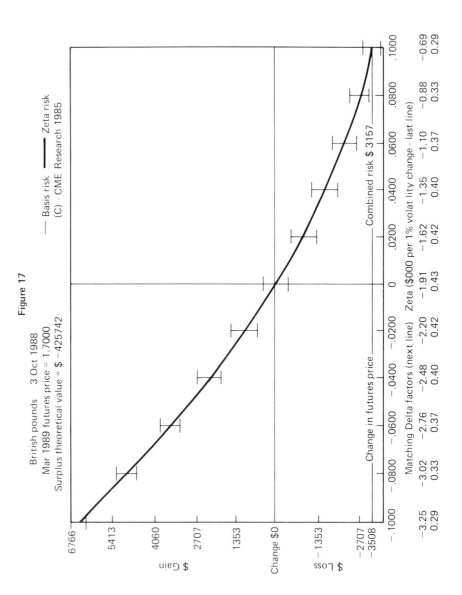

Figure 17

Figure 18

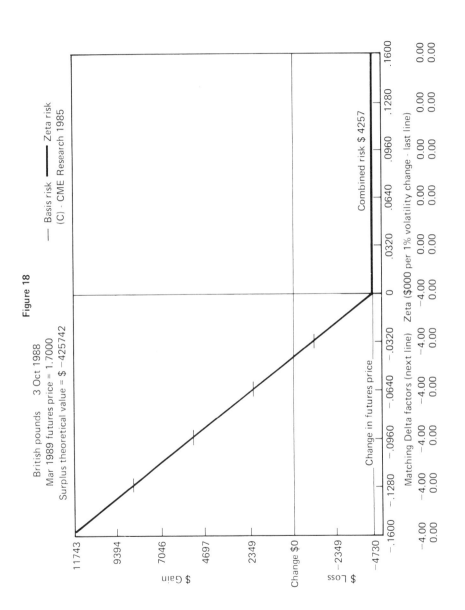

British pounds   3 Oct 1988
Mar 1989 futures price = 1.7000
Surplus theoretical value = $ −425742

How to construct

1. Sell a call in the market.
2. Sell the underlying currency and sell a put at the same time and with the same strike price as the current spot or forward rate.

The effects

1. If you are correct in your assumptions and the value of the underlying currency stagnates or depreciates –

   (a) The call will decrease in value allowing for it to be either purchased back at a lower cost, or expire worthless.
   (b) The put will increase in value and will be exercised, the writer of the put will apply the currency received on the exercise against the short underlying currency position and will retain the premium received as profit. Or, alternatively, repurchase the underlying currency at a lower rate than that at which it was sold and at the same time repurchase the short put position.

2. If you are incorrect and the value of the underlying currency appreciates –

   (a) The call will appreciate in value and will have to be repurchased at a loss or if exercised the underlying currency will have to be purchased in the spot market at a loss to meet the obligations under the option.
   (b) The short position in the underlying currency will immediately start to show losses as the value of the currency appreciates and, of course, the put sold will not be exercised by the holder because he will be able to achieve a better rate for the currency in the spot market. The only protection for the writer will be the premium originally received.

Profit and loss characteristics

1. Losses are unlimited and equate to Strike and Premium – underlying.
2. Profits are limited to the original premium received for selling the option.

See Figures 19 and 20 (page 78).

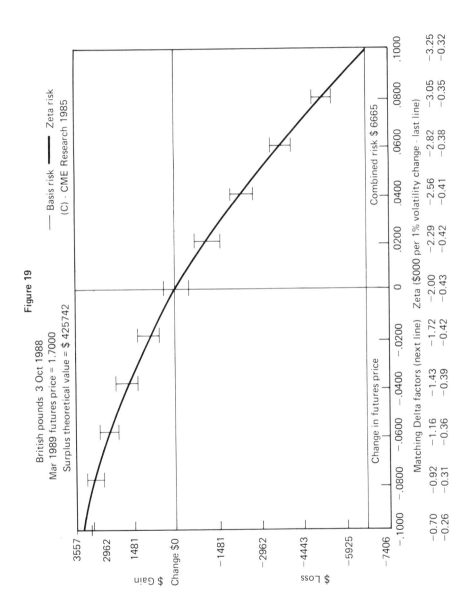

Figure 19

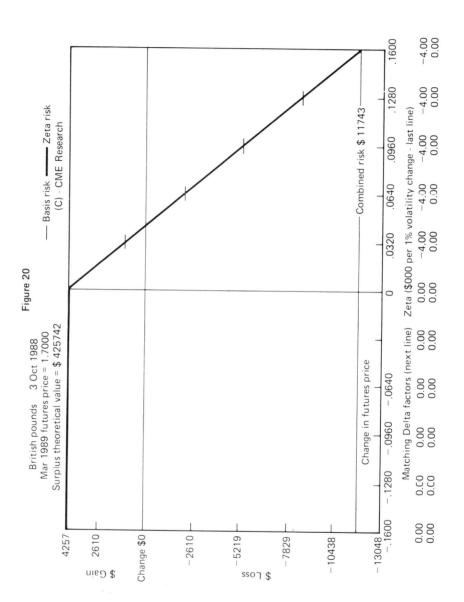

Figure 20

TYPE OF STRATEGY: Short Put Options

When to use

If you believe that the market will stagnate or rise in value and are prepared to take an unlimited risk for a limited reward i.e. the premiums received. The shorter the option period obviously the shorter the risk, but the higher the 'gammas' which can cause problems if the seller is delta hedging (see Chapter 8). Care should also be taken when writing options of a longer duration (unless the strategy is against income streams). It is quite possible to bear the risk for say five months of a six month option successfully and in the final month see a sharp move in the value of the underlying currency which will remove all the profit previously earned and create a loss before maturity.

How to construct

1. Sell a put in the market.
2. Buy the underlying currency and sell a call at the same strike price as the current spot or forward rate.

What are the effects

1. If you are correct in your assumptions and the value of the underlying currency does stagnate or appreciates in value –

   (a) The put will decrease in value allowing for it to be either purchased back at a lower cost or expire worthless.
   (b) The call will increase in value and will be exercised, the writer of the call will use the underlying currency purchased to meet the obligations under the option contract and will retain the premium received as profit. Alternatively, sell for a profit the underlying currencies purchased and at the same time buy back the short call option position.

2. If you are incorrect and the value of the underlying currency depreciates –

   (a) The put will appreciate and will have to be repurchased at a loss or if exercised the underlying currency will have to be sold in the spot market at a loss to meet the obligations under the option, or
   (b) The long position in the underlying currency will immediately start to show losses as the value of the currency depreciates and of course

the call sold will not be exercised by the holder because he will be able to achieve a better rate for the currency in the spot market. The only protection for the writer will be the premium originally received.

Profit and loss characteristics

1. Losses are unlimited and equate to the difference between the Strike minus the Premium and the underlying.
2. Profits are limited to the original premium received for selling the option.

See Figures 21 and 22 (pages 81 and 82).

TYPE OF STRATEGY: Bull Spread

When to use

If you believe that the value of the underlying currency is about to rise. This strategy allows for a limited risk and a limited profit potential, both of which can be adjusted to meet the expectations of the individual undertaking the strategy. If for example expectations are that the value of the underlying currency will rise significantly the following strategy could be used.

Current Pound to Dollar is 1.70 (1)

Note 1	Buy	1.70 Call	Cost cents	4.20
	Sell	1.75 Call	Income cents	2.30
	Potential gain	0.05	Cost of Strategy	1.90

Net Potential gain 3.10

Maximum Profit is Cents 3.10
Maximum Loss is   Cents 1.90

If expectations are that the rise will be smaller a strategy nearer the money is more appropriate e.g.

Note 1	Buy	1.65 Call	Cost cents	6.90
	Sell	1.70 Call	Income cents	4.20
	Potential gain	0.05	Cost of Strategy	2.70

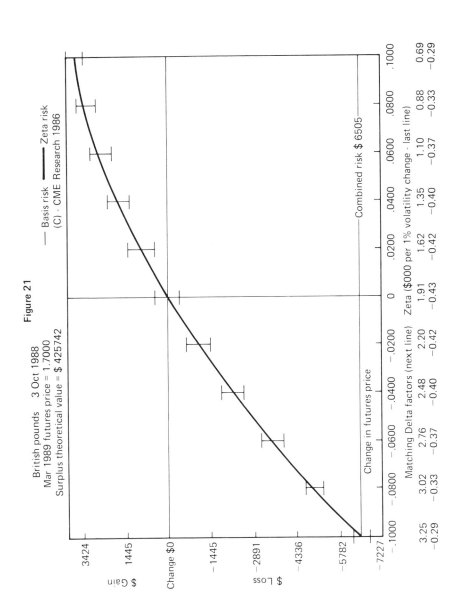

Figure 21

British pounds   3 Oct 1988
Mar 1989 futures price = 1.7000
Surplus theoretical value = $ 425742

— Basis risk ▬▬ Zeta risk
(C) - CME Research 1986

Combined risk $ 6505

Change in futures price

Matching Delta factors (next line)

Zeta ($000 per 1% volatility change - last line)

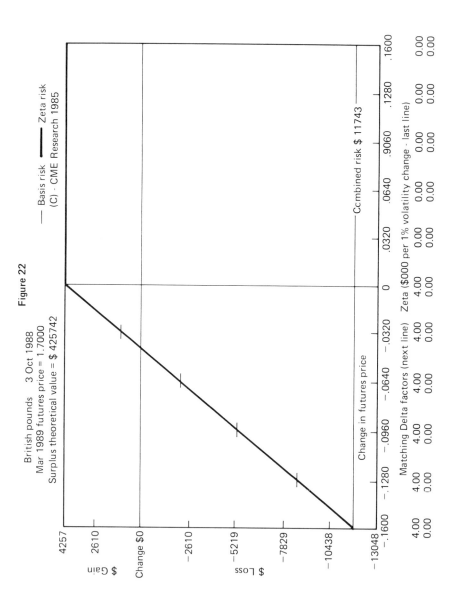

Figure 22

Net Potential gain 2.3

Maximum Profit is Cents 2.30
Maximum Loss is   Cents 2.70

The advantage that this type of strategy has over strategic positions in the Foreign Exchange Market is that it can be maintained even if the original expectations prove to be wrong in the early life of the strategy, thus overcoming the problems of being right in the direction of the underlying currency, but being taken out of a position because a sudden or unexpected drop in the value of the underlying currency causes a stop loss order to be executed.

How to construct

1. Buy Call 'A' Sell Call 'B'
2. Buy Put 'A' Sell Put 'B'

The effects

If you are correct in your assumptions and the value of the underlying currency appreciates in value Call 'A' which has been purchased will appreciate in value. Call 'B' (which has been sold) will also appreciate in value. Before a profit is achieved the value of the underlying currency at maturity must be at a level greater than 'A' plus the cost of the strategy. If the value of the underlying currency at maturity is less than 'A' plus the cost of the strategy a loss will be incurred. The loss will be limited to the original cost of the strategy.

Put 'A' (which has been purchased) will depreciate in value but because the original price was less than that of Put 'B' (which has been sold) it will leave a profit at maturity if the value of the underlying currency is at 'B' minus the income received for the original strategy. In the 'Put vs Put' version of this strategy Put 'B' must have a higher strike price than Put 'A' to generate income e.g.

Current Pound to Dollar rate 1.80 (1)

Note 1	Sell	1.85 Put	Income cent	8.15
	Buy	1.75 Put	Cost cent	2.27
	Potential loss	.10	Income cent	5.40

Maximum Profit cents 5.40
Maximum Loss cents 4.60

If the value of the underlying currency is less than 'B' minus the income received losses will be incurred. These losses are limited to the difference between 'A' and 'B' minus the income received.

Profit and loss characteristics

In all versions of this strategy, both profits and losses are limited. In the 'Call vs Call' version there is a cost in setting up the strategy. In 'Put vs Put' there is an income generated.

1. 'Call vs Call' losses are limited to the original cost of establishing the strategy. Profits are limited to the difference between 'A' and 'B' less the original cost of the strategy. Maximum profit is achieved if the value of the underlying currency is at or above the strike price of Call 'B'.
2. 'Put vs Put' profits are limited to the original income received and maximum profit is achieved if the value of the underlying currency is at or above the strike price of 'Put B'. Losses are limited to the difference between Strike 'A' and 'B' minus the original income received. Losses start to occur if the value of the underlying currency at maturity is at or below Strike 'B' minus the original income received.

See Figures 23 and 24 (pages 85 and 86).

TYPE OF STRATEGY: Bear Spread

When to use

If you believe that the value of the underlying currency is about to fall. This strategy allows for a limited risk and a limited profit potential both of which can be adjusted to meet the expectations of the individual undertaking the strategy. (See also the examples in Bull Spread).

How to construct

1. Buy Put 'B' Sell Put 'A'
2. Buy Call 'B' Sell Call 'A'

The effects

1. If you are correct in your assumptions and the value of the underlying currency depreciates, Put 'B' which has been purchased will appreciate

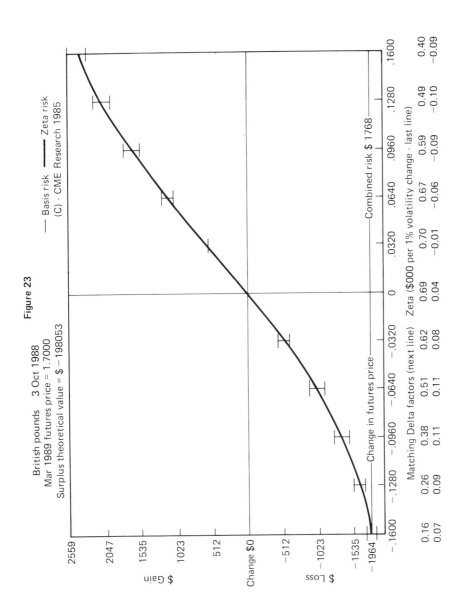

Figure 23

British pounds   3 Oct 1988
Mar 1989 futures price = 1.7000
Surplus theoretical value = $ −198053

— Basis risk —— Zeta risk
(C) - CME Research 1985

Figure 24

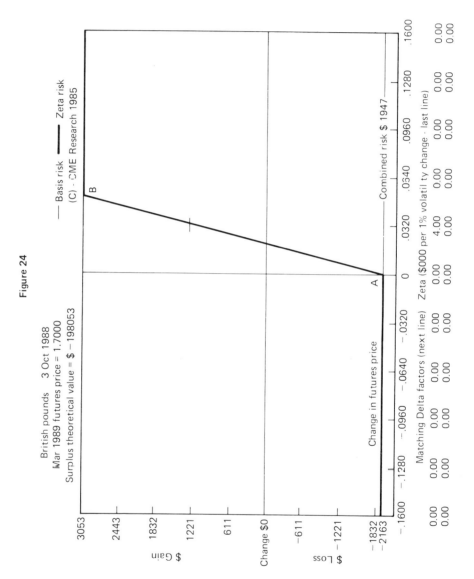

British pounds   3 Oct 1988
Mar 1989 futures price = 1.7000
Surplus theoretical value = $ -198053

in value, Put 'A' which has been sold will also appreciate in value. Before a profit is achieved the value of the underlying currency at maturity must be at a level which is less than Put 'B' minus the cost of the strategy. If the value of the underlying currency at maturity is greater than 'B' minus the cost of the strategy a loss will be incurred. The loss will be limited to the original cost of the strategy. If the value of the underlying currency is less than Put 'B' minus the cost of the strategy at maturity, profits start to accrue. The maximum profit is achieved at the strike price of Put 'A' and cannot exceed this amount.

Current Pound to Dollar rate 1.70

Sell	1.70 Put	Cost cents	4.20
Buy	1.65 Put	Income cents	2.30
Potential profit	0.5	Cost of Strategy cents	1.90

Maximum Profit cents	3.10
Maximum Loss cents	1.90

2. If you are correct in your assumptions and the value of the underlying currency depreciates, Call 'B' (which has been purchased) will depreciate in value but because the original price was less than that of Call 'A' (which has been sold) it will leave a profit at maturity if the value of the underlying currency is at a rate of 'B' minus the income received from the original strategy. If the underlying currency at maturity is greater than 'B' minus the income received, losses will be incurred. These losses are limited to the difference between 'A' and 'B' minus the income received.

Profit and loss characteristics

In all versions of this strategy both profits and losses are limited. In the 'Put vs Put' version there is a cost in setting up the strategy. In the 'Call vs Call' there is an income generated.

1. 'Put vs Put'. Losses are limited to the original cost of establishing the strategy. Profits are limited to the difference between 'A' and 'B' less the original cost of the strategy. Maximum profit is achieved if the value of the underlying currency at maturity is at below the strike price of Put 'A'.

2. 'Call vs Call'. Profits are limited to the original income received and maximum profit is achieved if the value of the underlying currency at maturity is at or below the strike price of Call 'A'. Losses are limited to the difference between Strike 'A' and Strike 'B' minus the original

income received. Losses start to occur if the value of the underlying currency at maturity is at or greater than Strike 'B' minus the original income received.

See Figures 25 and 26 (pages 89 and 90).

TYPE OF STRATEGY: Short Straddle

When to use

If you believe that the value of the underlying currency will stagnate or at least not move outside of two given exchange rates and are prepared to take an unlimited risk for a limited period.

How to construct

Sell Call 'A' and Sell Put 'A'

The effects

If you are correct in your assumptions and the value of the underlying currency at maturity is within a range of 'A' plus or minus the income received, you will make a profit. The maximum profit which can be achieved is if the value of the underlying currency moves in either direction away from 'A'. Losses start to accrue at 'A' minus or 'A' plus the income received from the original strategy and you are exercised on one of the two options sold. In the event that you are exercised before maturity on one of the options written, it is advisable to consider repurchasing the other option to stop further losses.

Profit and loss characteristics

Profits are limited to the original income received. As the value of the underlying currency moves away from 'A', profits decline and at maturity profits will be equal to the difference between 'A' plus or minus the value of the underlying currency less the original premium received.

Losses are unlimited and are equal to 'A' plus or minus the value of the underlying currency less the original premium received. See Figures 27 and 28 (pages 91 and 92).

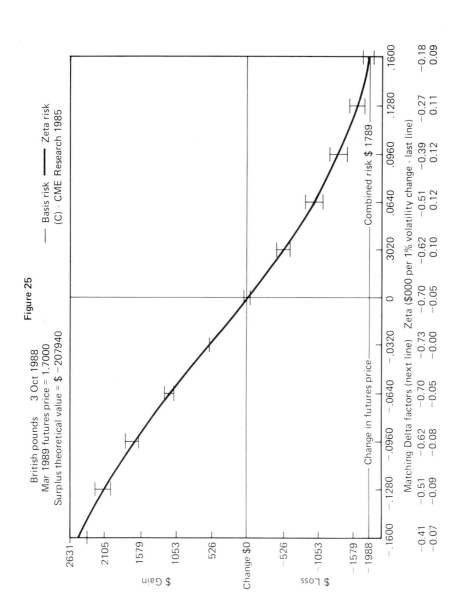

Figure 25

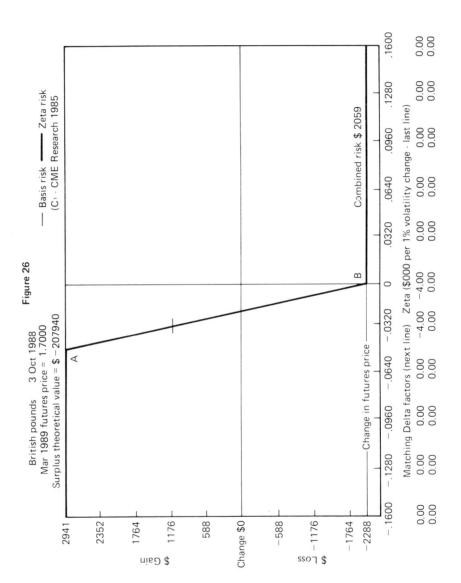

Figure 26

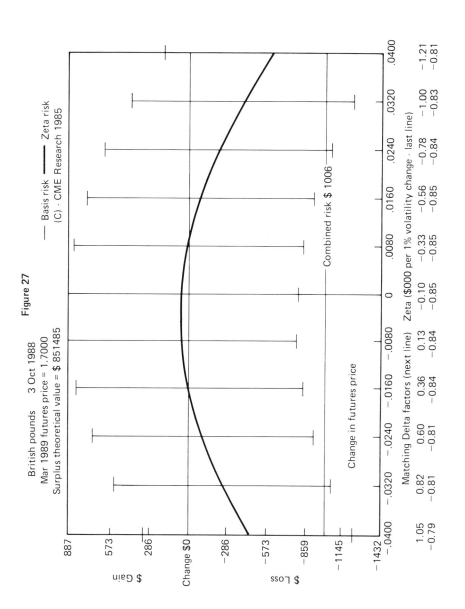

Figure 27

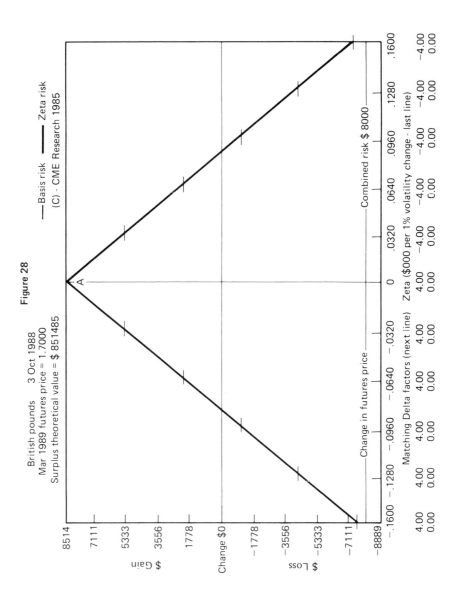

Figure 28

TYPE OF STRATEGY: Long Straddle

When to use

If you believe that the value of the underlying currency is about to move in a dramatic way but are not sure of the direction of the move, or if you believe that the value of the underlying currency could move dramatically in one direction and then reverse and move dramatically in the opposite direction.

How to construct

Buy Call 'A' Buy Put 'A'

The effects

If you are correct in your assumptions and the value of the underlying currency at maturity is greater than Call 'A' plus the original cost of the strategy or less than Put 'B' minus the cost of the strategy, you will achieve a profit. If the value of the underlying currency at maturity is greater than Call 'A' but less than Call 'A' plus the original cost of the strategy, Call 'A' must still be exercised but a loss will be incurred equal to the difference between the value of the underlying currency and Call 'A' plus the original cost. Similarly, if the value of the underlying currency at maturity is less than Put 'B' minus the original cost of the strategy, Put 'B' must still be exercised but a loss will be incurred equal to the difference between the value of the underlying currency and Put 'B' minus the original cost.

In the event that the value of the underlying currency moves quickly to a point where you have covered the cost of the original strategy and you expect the market to reverse, it could be profitable to sell off one side of the Straddle. It is not necessary for the value of the underlying to return to the strike price of the remaining option for you to profit because the cost of this option will have been taken into consideration when selling out the first leg of the Straddle and therefore to all intents the second leg is owned by you at no cost.

If you are incorrect in your assumptions and the value of the underlying currency does not appreciate to 'A' plus cost or depreciate to 'B' minus cost, a loss will be incurred. The maximum loss will be incurred if the value of the underlying currency at maturity is 'A' but the loss is limited to the original cost of the strategy. If at maturity the value of the underlying currency is below 'A' the put should be exercised. If it is greater than 'A' the call should be exercised.

Profit and loss characteristics

Profits are unlimited at 'A' minus or 'A' plus the cost of the strategy.

Losses are limited to the cost of the strategy.

It is unlikely that the value of the underlying currency will be at exactly 'A' at maturity and therefore it is essential to exercise the 'in the money' option at maturity.

This strategy can be expensive to construct because the buyer pays two premiums, one for the put and another for the call. It is therefore appropriate for the buyer of the strategy to calculate the cost of the strategy if currencies do not move as expected. This can be done by taking the premium paid and dividing it by the number of days in the period and writing off the cost over the life of the strategy. See Figures 29 and 30 (pages 95 and 96).

TYPE OF STRATEGY: Long Strangle

When to use

If you believe that the value of the underlying currency is about to move in a dramatic way but are not sure of the direction of the move, or if you believe that the value of the underlying currency could move dramatically in one direction and then reverse and move dramatically in the opposite direction. The difference between this strategy and a Long Straddle is that because you are purchasing two options which are 'out of the money' as opposed to 'at the money' the strategy will be cheaper to construct. The downside of this is that the value of the underlying currency will have to have moved further away from its original value for you to profit. Your expectation of movement should be compared to the cost of a Straddle and a Strangle to see which one gives the overall best profit potential after having taken account of the cost of the strategy.

How to construct

(1) Buy Call 'B' Buy Put 'A'
(2) Buy Call 'A' Buy Put 'B'

In the case of (2) because you are buying in the money options the amount of time value which you pay is less than with a Straddle.

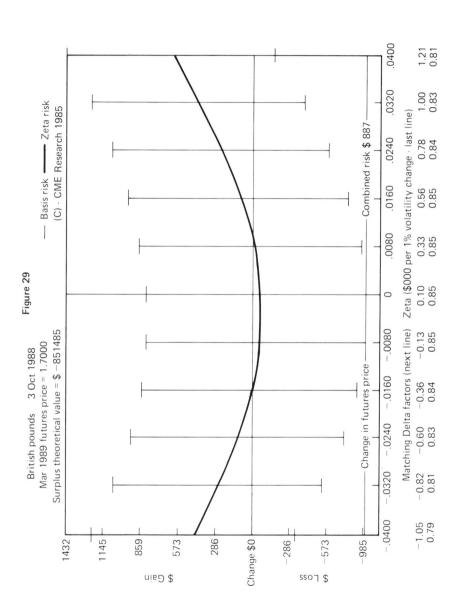

Figure 29

British pounds   3 Oct 1988
Mar 1989 futures price = 1.7000
Surplus theoretical value = $ −851485

— Basis risk   ▬▬ Zeta risk
(C) - CME Research 1985

Combined risk $ 887

Change in futures price

Matching Delta factors (next line)

Zeta ($000 per 1% volatility change - last line)

	−.0400	−.0320	−.0240	−.0160	−.0080	0	.0080	.0160	.0240	.0320	.0400
Delta	−1.05	−0.82	−0.60	−0.36	−0.13	0.10	0.33	0.56	0.78	1.00	1.21
Zeta	0.79	0.81	0.83	0.84	0.85	0.85	0.85	0.85	0.84	0.83	0.81

$ Gain
1432
1145
859
573
286
Change $0
−286
−573
−985
$ Loss

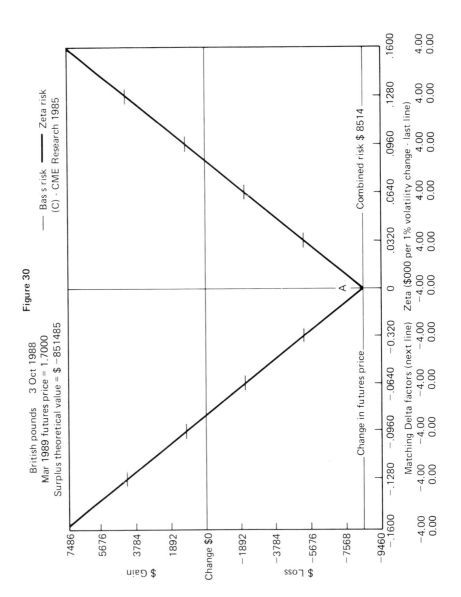

Figure 30

The effects

1. If you are correct in your assumptions and the value of the underlying currency changes dramatically you will start to profit at 'A' minus or 'B' plus the cost of the original strategy. The maximum loss is the original cost of the strategy and is incurred if the value of the underlying currency remains in a band between 'A' and 'B'. Profits are unlimited if the value of the underlying currency goes beyond 'A' minus or 'B' plus the cost of the underlying currency.
2. In the case of purchasing both a put and a call which are 'in the money', if the currency moves at all in either direction you will see exchange gains which will offset the amount of time premium which you pay for this strategy. The initial cost of purchasing an 'in the money' Strangle will be greater than the purchase of an 'out of the money' Strangle.

Therefore your maximum loss on this strategy is not the whole premium paid but only the time value paid. The maximum loss is incurred between 'A' and 'B'. If the value of the underlying currency is below 'A' or above 'B' at maturity loss decline, profits start at 'B' minus or 'A' plus the time value paid and are unlimited beyond this point.

Profit and loss characteristics

Profits are unlimited and in

  1. are 'A' minus the cost or 'B' plus the cost of the original strategy, and
  2. are 'A' plus or 'B' minus the original time value paid.

Losses are limited and in

  1. are limited to the original cost of the strategy, and
  2. are limited to the original time value paid.

See Figures 31 and 32 (pages 98 and 99).

TYPE OF STRATEGY: Short Strangle

When to use

If you believe that the value of the underlying currency will remain within two specific exchange rates and are willing to take an unlimited risk for a limited profit potential.

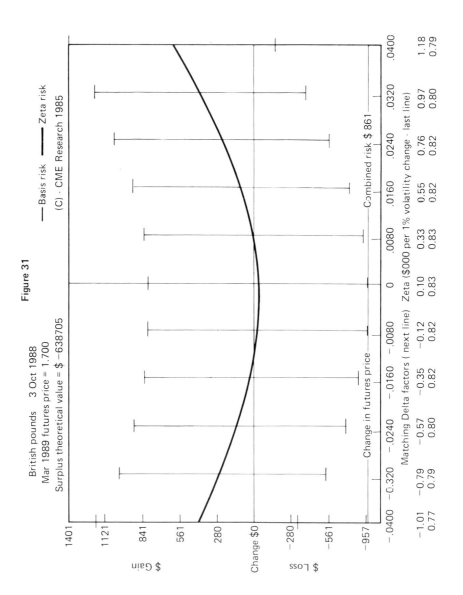

Figure 31

British pounds   3 Oct 1988
Mar 1989 futures price = 1.700
Surplus theoretical value = $ -638705

——— Basis risk ——— Zeta risk
(C) - CME Research 1985

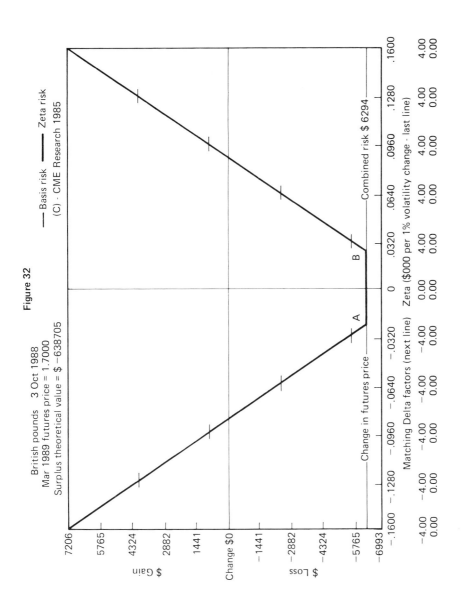

Figure 32

How to construct

1. Sell Put 'A' Sell Call 'B'
2. Sell Call 'A' Sell Put 'B'

The effects

1. If you are correct in your assumptions and the value of the underlying currency at maturity is between 'A' and 'B' you will profit by the maximum amount which is the original income received for selling the strategy. Profits continue to the point of 'A' minus or 'B' plus the income originally received. Losses start to accrue beyond this point and are unlimited. As is the case with the 'Short Straddle' if you receive early exercise on one of the options written, consideration should be given to closing out the remaining leg as a stop loss precaution.
2. In this version of the strategy you are selling two 'in the money options' and therefore can expect to be exercised on one or other leg at maturity, i.e. if the value of the underlying currency is greater than 'A' at maturity the call will be exercised and if the value of the underlying currency is less than 'B' the put will be exercised, and if the value of the underlying is between 'A' and 'B' you will be exercised on both options. Therefore the maximum profit is the 'time value' received which can be calculated by taking 'A' from 'B' and then subtracting the result from the premium received. Losses are unlimited and start to accrue at 'B' minus or 'A' plus the original time value received.

Profit and loss characteristics

Profits are limited and in

1. are equal to the original premiums received, and
2. are equal to the original time value received.

Losses are unlimited and in

1. start to be incurred at 'A' minus or 'B' plus the original premium received, and
2. start to be incurred at 'B' minus or 'A' plus the original time value received.

NB: If the value of the underlying currency is between 'A' and 'B' at maturity and you are exercised on both, then you have achieved your maximum profit objective, but if you receive an early exercise on one leg of the strategy which you close out in the spot FX market, to close out your second exercise the loss will, in all probability, be more than the original time value received.

See Figures 33 and 34 (page 102).

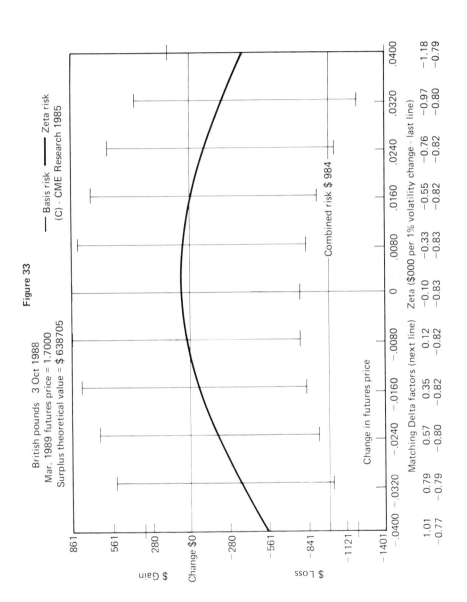

Figure 33

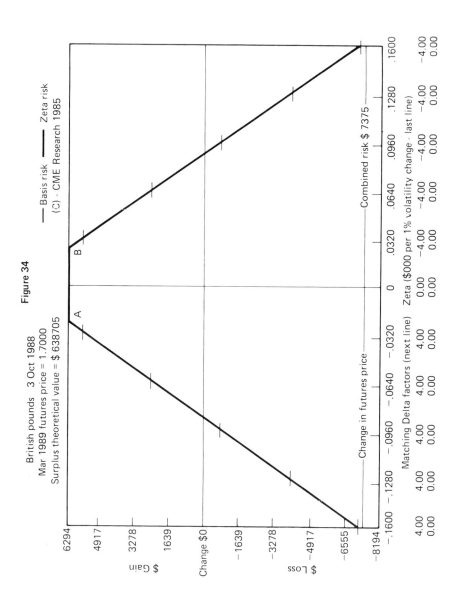

Figure 34

British pounds   3 Oct 1988
Mar 1989 futures price = 1.7000
Surplus theoretical value = $ 638705

Basis risk ——— Zeta risk
(C) - CME Research 1985

TYPE OF STRATEGY: Ratio Call Spread

When to use

If you believe that the value of the underlying currency will appreciate from 'A' but is unlikely to go beyond point 'B'.

How to construct

Purchase Call 'A'. Sell Calls 'B'

The number of calls sold at Strike Price 'B' will depend upon how confident you are that the value of the underlying currency will not appreciate before 'B'.

It is usual to construct this strategy to original delta neutrality thereby causing the strategy to incur a small cost to construct but reducing the risk and potential loss if the value of the underlying currency appreciates beyond 'B'. The example shown is constructed by buying one call 'A' and selling two calls 'B'.

The effects

If you are correct in your assumptions and the value of the underlying currency at maturity is near to point 'B', Call 'A' will have appreciated in value but the Calls 'B' which have been sold will not be exercisable or may only be exercisable for a modest profit by the buyer. The income received from selling Calls 'B' has been utilised to offset the cost of purchasing Call 'A'. In the event that the value of the underlying currency is less than 'A' at maturity the loss is limited to the original cost of the strategy. If the value of the underlying currency is greater than 'B' at maturity you will have a greater number of calls making losses than those which are making profits for you but the decline in profit is less abrupt because you will have a locked in profit of the difference between 'A' and 'B' to offset the original cost of the strategy and any losses incurred because of calls written in excess of those purchased.

Profit and loss characteristics

Profits are limited and are equal to 'B' minus 'A' minus the original cost of the strategy with maximum profit achieved at 'B'. Breakeven is achieved at 'A' plus the cost of the strategy.

Losses are:

1. Limited if the value of the underlying currency at maturity is less than 'A' and are equal to the original cost of the strategy.
2. Unlimited if the value of the underlying currency at maturity is greater than 'B' plus the profit earned between 'A' and 'B' less the original cost of the strategy. The extent to which profits are offset by losses depend on the ratio of calls written to calls purchased e.g.

Purchased £1 million) = losses
Sold   £3 million)   of USD 20 000/cent 1 move

These losses will be added to the original cost of the strategy and offset against profit earned by the difference between 'A' and 'B' on the call 'A' purchased. See Figures 35 and 36 (pages 105 and 106).

TYPE OF STRATEGY: Ratio Put Spread

When to use

If you believe that the value of the underlying currency will depreciate from point 'B' but is unlikely to go beyond point 'A'.

How to construct

Purchase Put 'B' Sell Puts 'A'

The number of puts sold at Strike Price 'A' will depend on how confident you are that the value of the underlying currency will not depreciate beyond 'A'.

It is usual to construct this strategy to original delta neutrality thereby causing the strategy to incur a small cost to construct but reducing the risk and potential loss if the value of the underlying currency depreciates beyond 'A'.

The effects

If you are correct in your assumptions and the value of the underlying currency at maturity has depreciated from 'B' to near 'A' the Put 'B' which you have purchased will have appreciated in value but the ratio of Puts 'A' which you sold will not be exercisable because they are only at the money or they will be exercisable by the holder for a modest profit. The income received from selling Puts 'A' has been utilised to offset the cost of purchasing Put 'B'. If the value of the underlying currency at maturity is greater than 'B' the loss is limited to the original cost of the strategy. If the

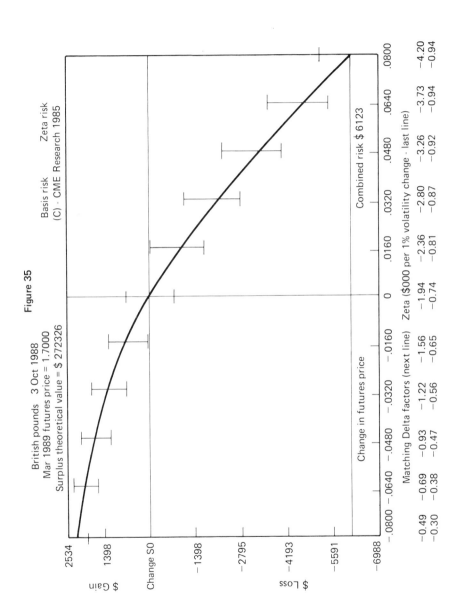

Figure 35

British pounds   3 Oct 1988
Mar 1989 futures price = 1.7000
Surplus theoretical value = $ 272326

Basis risk   Zeta risk
(C) - CME Research 1985

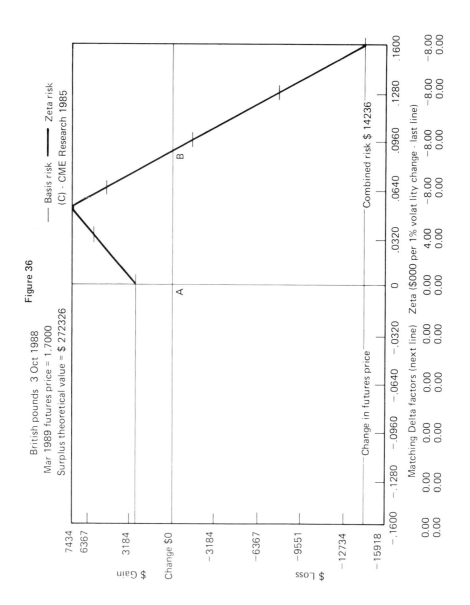

Figure 36

value of the underlying currency at maturity is less than 'A' you will have a greater number of puts making losses than those which are making profits for you but the decline in profits is less abrupt because you will have a locked in profit of the difference between 'B' and 'A' on the put purchased to offset the original cost of the strategy and any losses incurred in writing more puts than have been purchased.

The profit decline becomes more pronounced the greater the number of options written in excess of those purchased.

Profit and loss characteristics

Profits are limited and are equal to 'B' minus 'A' minus the original cost of the strategy with the maximum profit being achieved at 'A'. Breakeven occurs if the value of the underlying currency at maturity is at 'B' minus the original cost of the strategy.

Losses are:

(a) Limited if the value of the underlying currency at maturity is greater than 'B' and are equal to the original cost of the strategy.
(b) Unlimited if the value of the underlying currency at maturity is less than 'A' minus the cost of the original strategy minus the profit earned between 'B' and 'A', then losses are incurred by the excess amount of puts sold over puts purchased.

See Figures 37 and 38 (pages 108 and 109).

TYPE OF STRATEGY: Short Butterfly

When to use

If you believe that the value of the underlying currency will remain within a range of A to C less the cost of originating the strategy, and you wish to have a limited risk if your assumptions are wrong. This strategy is helped by a decrease in volatility.

How to constuct

Purchase 1 Call A	or	Purchase 1 Put C
Sell 2 × Call B (Call version)		Sell 2 × Put B (Put version)
Purchase 1 Call C		Purchase 1 Put A

NB: A and C must be equidistant to B to equalise the effect of the underlying in an up or down market.

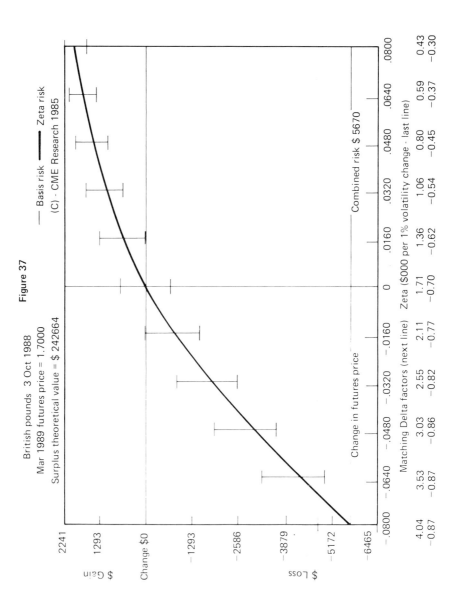

Figure 37

British pounds 3 Oct 1988
Mar 1989 futures price = 1.7000
Surplus theoretical value = $ 242664

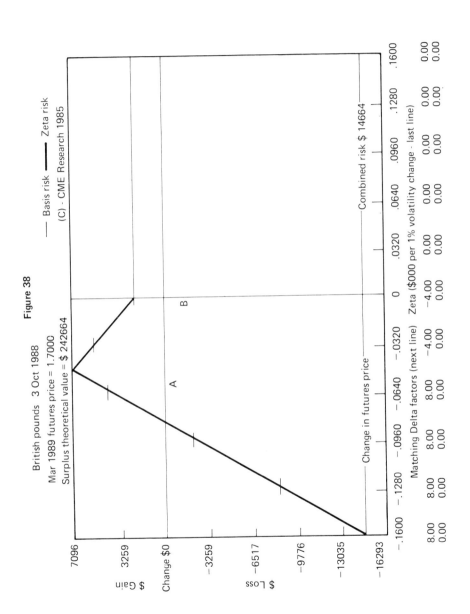

Figure 38

The effects

If you are incorrect in your assumptions and the value of the underlying at maturity is below A, all calls (in the call version) expire worthless. If the value is between A and B but not above B, call A is exercised. If the underlying value is between B and C, but not above C, calls A and B are exercised. If the value of the underlying is above C all options are exercised.

In the put version if the value of the underlying is above C, all options expire worthless. If it is between C and B, puts C are exercised. At a level between A and B, puts C and B are both exercised. Finally if the value of the underlying is below A, all options are exercised.

The profit and loss characteristics

Both profits and losses are limited with the maximum profit being achieved if the value of the underlying at maturity is equal to strike price B. It is usual to execute this transaction as a debit spread (i.e. have to pay a net premium to instigate the trade. If it were possible to be able to implement this strategy for a credit it would signify that either an arbitrage is in existence (unlikely), or A and C are not equidistant to B, in which case a true butterfly does not exist).

If at maturity the value of the underlying is less than A, all options expire worthless and the loss is limited to the original cost of the strategy. Once the value of the underlying has appreciated to a point equal to A plus the original cost of the strategy, breakeven has been achieved. Profits continue to accrue up to but not beyond B. The profit at point B is equal to A minus B, minus the original cost of the strategy. Profits start to decline beyond point B down to a breakeven of C, minus the cost of the original strategy. At point C the maximum loss, i.e. the original cost of the strategy, is incurred and remains constant beyond point C.

Losses at lower than a rate of A or higher than a rate of C are equal so long as A $-$ B $=$ B $-$ C.

The above relates to the call version. To simulate the profit and loss profile of the puts version: buy put C, sell 2 $\times$ Put B, and buy put A. Then track the path of the underlying as it moves down from say, 1.80 to 1.60. The basic rules of limited loss still apply if equidistant strike intervals are used. See Figures 39 and 40 (page 112).

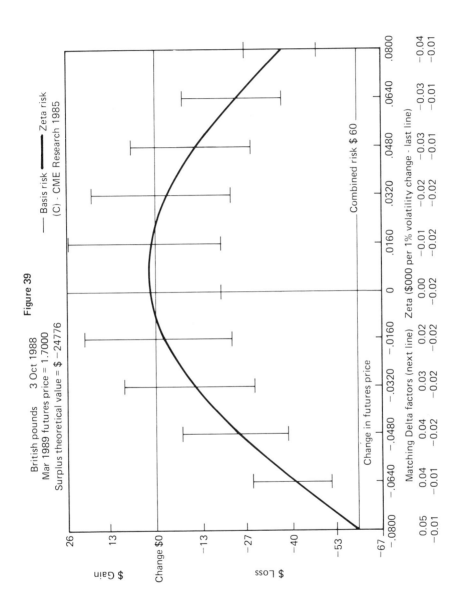

Figure 39

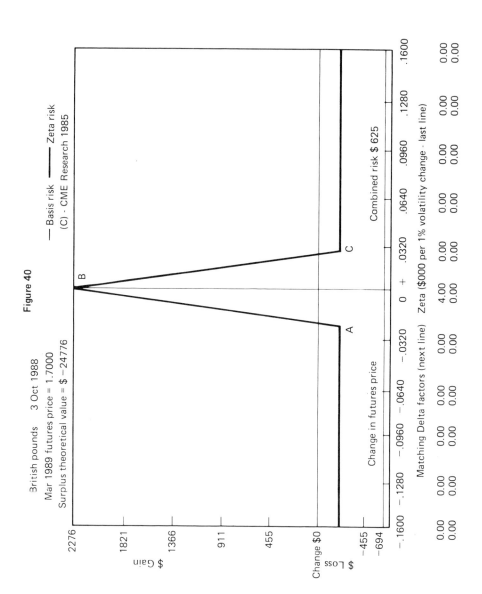

Figure 40

TYPE OF STRATEGY: Long Butterfly

When to use

If you believe that the value of the underlying currency will move away from its current value but are unsure in which direction. Losses and profits are limited, judgement should be used when assessing the risk reward ratio. This strategy is helped by an increase in volatility.

How to construct

Sell 1 Call A
Buy 2 × Call B (Call version)
Sell 1 × Call C

or

Sell 1 Put C
Buy 2 × Put B (Put version)
Sell 1 Put A

NB: Both Calls A and C and Puts A and C should be equidistant to Call B (in the call version) and put B (in the put version).

The effects

If you are correct in your assumptions and in the case of the call version the value of the underlying currency moves up beyond a point equal to C minus the original income received, the maximum profit potential is achieved. This profit is equal to the profit achieved if the value of the underlying currency falls beyond a point equal to A plus the original income received between these two points, i.e. where there is very little change in the value of the underlying currency, losses are incurred, the maximum loss being at point B.

In the case of the put version the same rules apply.

Profit and loss characteristics

In the call version if at maturity the value of the underlying currency is at or below A, the maximum profit is equal to the original cost for constructing the strategy. In this case all options expire worthless. As the value of the underlying currency rises beyond point A the profit declines, breakeven being a rate equal to A plus the original premium received. See Figures 41 and 42 (page 115).

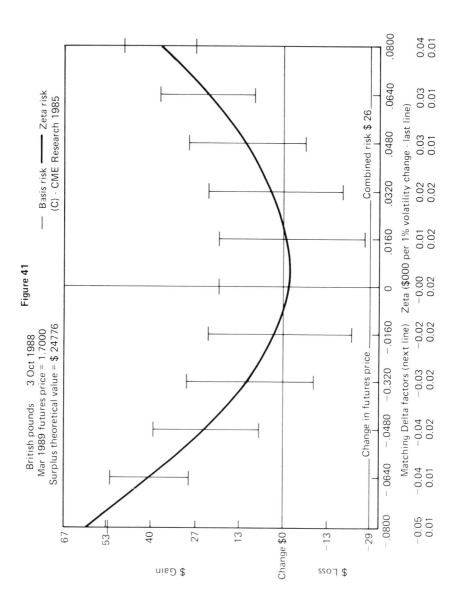

Figure 41

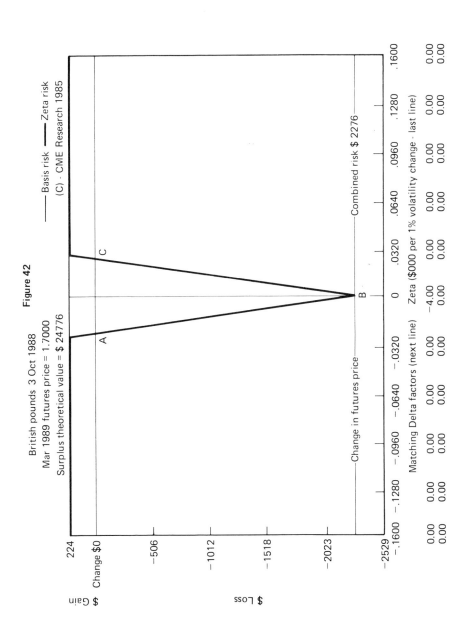

Figure 42

British pounds 3 Oct 1988
Mar 1989 futures price = 1.7000
Surplus theoretical value = $ 24776

Basis risk ——— Zeta risk
(C) - CME Research 1985

TYPE OF STRATEGY: Call Ratio Backspread

When to use

If you believe that the value of the underlying currency will appreciate but wish to limit your losses if it does not.

How to construct

Sell 1 × Call A
Purchase 2 × Call B

The effects

If you are incorrect in your assumptions and the value of the underlying currency falls, the loss is limited. If at maturity the value of the underlying currency is below strike price A, no options are exercised and loss is limited to the original debit incurred in constructing the strategy. It is possible but not usual to create a ratio backspread as a credit strategy but if this approach is undertaken it deepens the maximum loss 'V' and therefore requires a commensurately larger move up in the value of the underlying to breakeven. This occurs because a deep in-the-money option is being sold to finance the at-the-money options purchased. If at maturity the value of the underlying is above A but below B, call option A is exercised giving rise to a loss equal to the original debit plus the difference between A and the value of the underlying. The maximum loss is occurred at point B. If the value of the underlying at maturity is above B, the maximum loss declines until breakeven is achieved at B plus the difference between A and B and the original debit incurred. At a point where the underlying is greater than B, all options are exercised.

The profit and loss characteristics

Losses are limited, the greatest loss occurring at strike price B. Above a point which is equal to strike price B, plus the differences between A and B, plus the original cost of the strategy, the holder has the equivalent of a long position in the underlying currency.

The effect of increases in volatility help, slowing down the decay of the premium. Decreases in volatility hurt accelerating the time decay. This is so because the strategy requires the sale of intrinsic value to purchase extrinsic (i.e. time and volatility) value. See Figures 43 and 44 (page 118).

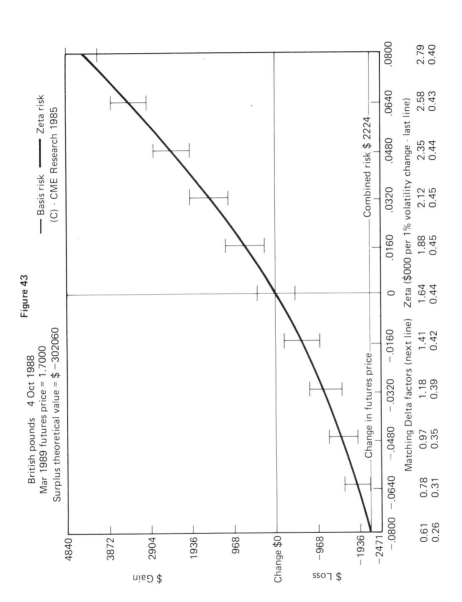

Figure 43

British pounds   4 Oct 1988
Mar 1989 futures price = 1.7000
Surplus theoretical value = $ −302060

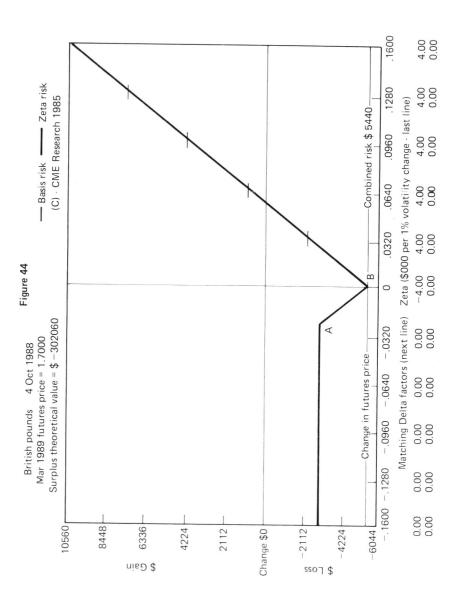

Figure 44

TYPE OF STRATEGY: Put Ratio Backspread

When to use

If you believe that the value of the underlying currency will fall in value but wish to limit your losses if it does not.

How to construct

Sell 1 × Put B
Purchase 2 × Put A

The effects

If you are incorrect in your assumptions and the value of the underlying currency rises, the loss is limited. If at maturity the value of the underlying currency is at a point greater than strike price B, no options are exercised and the loss is limited to the original debit incurred in constructing the strategy. It is possible but not usual to create a ratio backspread since as a credit spread it deepens the maximum loss 'V' and therefore requires a commensurately larger move down in the value of the underlying to break even. This occurs because a deep in-the-money option is being sold to finance the at-the-money options purchased.

If at maturity the value of the underlying currency is below B but above A, put option B is exercised giving rise to a loss equal to the original debit plus the difference between B and the value of the underlying currency. The maximum loss is incurred at A. If the value of the underlying currency at maturity is below A, the maximum loss declines until breakeven is achieved at A, minus the difference between B and A, plus the original debit incurred. At a point where the underlying is less than A, all options are exercised.

The profit and loss characteristics

Losses are limited, the greatest loss occuring at strike price A. Below a point which is equal to A, minus the difference between A–C, plus the original strategy, the holder has the equivalent of a short position in the underlying currency.

The effect of increases in volatility help, slowing down the effect of decay of the premiums. Decreases in volatility hurt accelerating the effects of the decay. This is because the strategy requires the sale of intrinsic value to purchase extrinsic (i.e. time and volatility) value. See Figures 45 and 46 (page 121).

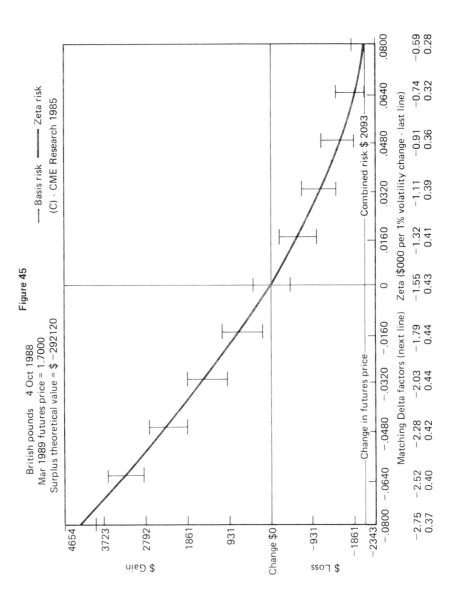

Figure 45

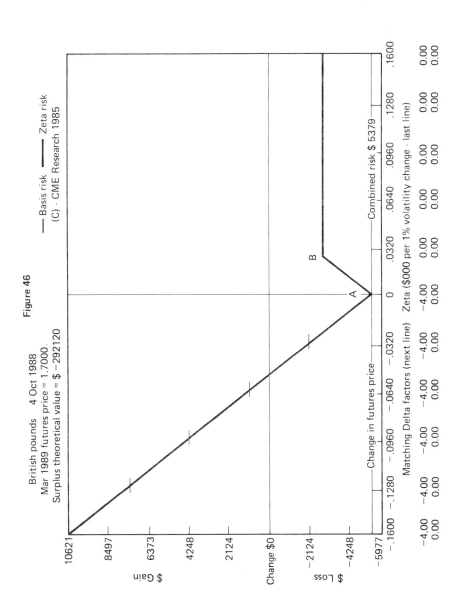

Figure 46

British pounds   4 Oct 1988
Mar 1989 futures price = 1.7000
Surplus theoretical value = $ -292120

Basis risk ——— Zeta risk
(C) - CME Research 1985

TYPE OF STRATEGY: Call Christmas Tree

When to use

If you believe that the value of the underlying currency will appreciate but to a limited extent and are prepared to accept an unlimited loss if the value of the underlying currency continues to appreciate beyond the point which was envisaged.

How to construct

Purchase 1 × Call A
Sell 1 × Call B
Sell 1 × Call C

The effects

If you are correct in your assumptions and the value of the underlying currency appreciates you will profit up to a maximum point equal to strike price B. At a rate equal to strike price B, and up to strike price C, profit remains constant. If at maturity the value of the underlying currency is greater than C, profit declines equal to a short position in the underlying.

If at maturity the value of the underlying currency is less than A, the profit is limited to the original credit received for creating the strategy. At a point which is less than A, all options expire worthless. The distance between A, B and C is normally equidistant.

The profit and loss characteristics

Losses and profits are mixed, a value of the underlying currency at maturity which is less than strike price A will give rise to a profit equal to the nett results of all of the premium.

The profit rises up to a maximum level of B where profit equals the difference between A and B, plus the original credit received (assuming that the strategy was undertaken for a credit). Profit remains constant up to C where all options are exercised. This will give rise to the equivalent position of a short position in the underlying. Breakeven is reached when the underlying reaches a point greater than C, minus the sum of A − B, plus the original credit.

The attraction of this type of strategy is that whilst losses are not limited a substantial appreciation of the underlying is required before losses are incurred. See Figures 47 and 48 (page 124).

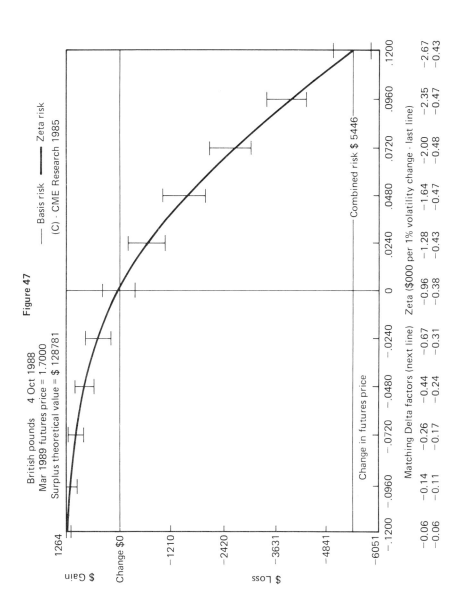

Figure 47

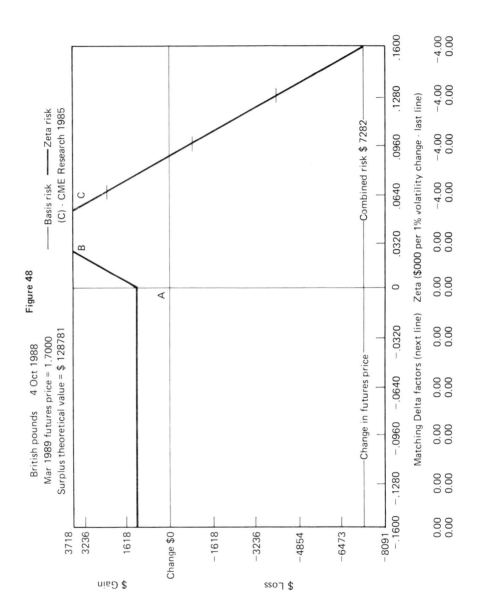

Figure 48

The following two tables show the theoretical fair value of the calls and puts and the requisite delta, gamma, theta and vegas.

TABLE: CALL DERIVATIVES

Futures Price 170.00	Estimated Volatility 10.0%	Interest Rate 8.0%	Start Date 10.03.1988		Expiration Date 03.10.1988
			Derivatives		
Strike Price	Theoretical Premium	Delta	Gamma	Theta	Vega
182.50	0.80	14.3%	2.0%	0.008	0.250
180.00	1.18	19.5%	2.4%	0.010	0.304
177.50	1.70	25.7%	2.8%	0.011	0.355
175.00	2.38	33.0%	3.2%	0.013	0.397
172.50	3.24	41.1%	3.4%	0.013	0.423
170.00	4.31	49.6%	3.4%	0.014	0.431
167.50	5.59	58.1%	3.3%	0.013	0.417
165.00	7.09	66.3%	3.1%	0.012	0.383
162.50	8.79	73.8%	2.7%	0.011	0.333
160.00	10.67	80.2%	2.2%	0.009	0.273
157.50	12.71	85.4%	1.7%	0.007	0.211
155.00	15.00	89.3%	1.2%	0.005	0.154

Date: 10.03.1988   Contract: British Pound 03/89

TABLE: PUT DERIVATIVES

Futures Price *170.00*	*Estimated Volatility* *10.0%*	*Interest Rate* *8.0%*	*Start Date* *10.03.1988*		*Expiration Date* *03.10.1988*

Strike Price	*Theoretical Premium*	*Delta*	*Gamma*	*Theta*	*Vega*
			Derivatives		
182.50	12.88	82.3%	2.0%	0.011	0.250
180.00	10.84	77.1%	2.4%	0.012	0.304
177.50	8.94	70.8%	2.8%	0.013	0.355
175.00	7.20	63.6%	3.2%	0.014	0.397
172.50	5.65	55.5%	3.4%	0.014	0.423
170.00	4.31	47.0%	3.4%	0.014	0.431
167.50	3.18	38.5%	3.3%	0.013	0.417
165.00	2.26	30.3%	3.1%	0.011	0.383
162.50	1.55	22.8%	2.7%	0.009	0.333
160.00	1.01	16.4%	2.2%	0.007	0.273
157.50	0.63	11.2%	1.7%	0.004	0.211
155.00	0.37	7.3%	1.2%	0.002	0.154

Date: 10.03.1988   Contract: British Pound 03/89

Chapter 7

Assumptions of the Formula

There are a number of formulae which are used in calculating prices for currency options. It is not intended to try and analyse every aspect of each and therefore for a more advanced discourse see Smith, *Trading Financial Options*. The aim of this chapter is to try and explain how and why the formulae are used and what problems exist if they are followed blindly. It was pointed out earlier in the book that currency options are believed to be 75% science and 25% art. For this reason one could encounter problems by slavishly adhering to the formulae.

THE FORMULA FOR CALCULATING HISTORICAL VOLATILITY

Historical volatility is the measure of the daily volatility of exchange rates and tells you what to expect for future exchange rate volatility if the pattern for the near future closely resembles the recent past. It is calculated by taking the exchange rate for two currencies at the same time each day and working out a ten, thirty or sixty day historical volatility. You are not limited to these three periods, you can choose any period which you feel is more relevant. It is also possible to weight the most recent past more heavily than the distant past if you feel that what happened yesterday is more important that what happened, say, thirty or sixty days ago. There are two important factors to be taken into consideration when using the formula for historical volatility, namely, you are taking no account of intra-day volatility and you are also unable to trade in historical volatility.

Does intra-day volatility matter and if so why?

The answer is yes, it does matter because exchange rates certainly move during the course of the business day and if you are responsible for hedging an option portfolio you will be aware of the intra-day movements. A check on the number of points between the day's high and low rates compared to the difference between day to day closing rates will show you that the former is normally greater than the latter. If conventional wisdom indicates that the portfolio is rehedged (in delta cash terms) at the same time as the rates are recorded to measure historical volatility you should not be rehedging more than once a day. This scenario is acceptable for a portfolio which is hedged predominantly options against options with a small amount of cash being used for fine tuning, but it certainly does not work if you are writing options and just delta hedging with cash or futures.

The fact that you are not able to trade historical volatility is important because historical volatility is only a measure of what has happened in the past and the real measure of an option's worth is the implied volatility contained in a live option quote.

Take for example the case of Sterling volatility in the run up to a UK Budget. This may or may not contain any surge in volatility as a result of the unexpected happening. Historical volatility does have some worth as a measure but common sense should be applied when either buying or selling options on the basis of the gap between historical and implied. Another example of where historical volatility can be misleading is again in Sterling, where implied volatility normally trades above historical volatility. From this one might assume that it is safe to sell options and delta hedge in the futures market. If one undertook this exercise it might prove profitable for a while but when Sterling moves it has a propensity to do so by one or two cents. Therefore, your daily income might be ten points and this amount and more could be lost in one go because of the jump effect.

Put/call parity is important in options pricing because it provides the means by which the calls, the puts and the cash or futures are related.

PUT CALL PARITY

If you think that an option is trading out of line, try the put call parity test e.g. if you think that the call is priced too expensively can you write it, buy the put, buy the cash and be left with a positive answer?

1.70 Call written	Received	cents 3.00 +
1.70 Put purchased	Pay	cents 3.50 −
1.70 Cash purchased	Receive	
	fwd swap	cents 0.50 +

Don't forget the early exercise factor may cause you to lose some of your swap points. In addition, you may have a negative carry cost on cash flow because of early exercise.

Call at 1.70 for £1 mio is exercised early therefore it is necessary to buy and sell £1 mio at current rates of 1.80. Therefore, cash flow funding cost is equal to the difference in price of the original strike price and the current spot replacement deal.

Call exercise at 1.70 with current spot at 1.80, the cash flows are as follows:

Call exercise	− £1 000 000	+ USD 1 700 000
Spot side of swap	+ £1 000 000	− USD 1 800 000
	NIL	− USD 100 000

The cash flow deficit has to be financed at current interest rates from the date of early exercise to the date of the original forward contract.

The formula for calculating the fair price of an option

The original formula for calculating option prices was devised by Fisher Black and Myron Scholes. It is based on the assumption that a synthetic option position can be created by utilising positions in the underlying currency, currency borrowing and deposits. The first assumption that is made is that the holder of an option will always exercise the option if at maturity it is in the money and not exercise the option if it is out of the money. Therefore, at maturity the option writer must own a position in the underlying currency equal to either 100% or 0% of the original option sold. These two assumptions are perfectly reasonable but it is, of course, the journey to maturity which is the difficult part to achieve. It is pointless to purchase, say, £1 mio in cover of a GBP 1.70 call written at a rate of 1.80 if the premium received for writing the option was only US cents 2.00, i.e.

Call written	1.70 +
Spot purchase	1.80 −
Premium received	0.02 +
	0.08 Unrelieved loss

Professors Black and Scholes set out to solve the problem of when to purchase positions in the underlying currency (either long or short positions) and how much to purchase. Their problem can be stated graphically. What they needed to do was find a way to predict the shape of the delta curve for any particular option e.g.

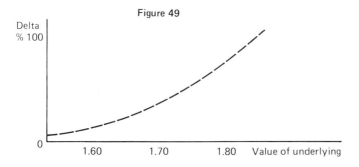

Figure 49

To assist them with their task they used statistical analysis and made a number of assumptions about the way the foreign exchange markets behave.

Random walk theory

The assumption that the markets follow a random walk mode was made. This means that the next market move can equally be up or down and that direction is not important. Random walk also assumes that each change in the value of the underlying currency is a tradable move with large deviations consisting of a number of small steps at each of which it is possible to execute trades in the underlying currency. There are problems in this assumption which could give rise to losses if delta hedging using futures is undertaken. The three most obvious problems are:

(a) the bid offer spread;
(b) the de-facto small size and number of trades which would need to be undertaken; and perhaps the most important of all
(c) the assumption that prices in the underlying currency move in an orderly and rational way.

Let us examine these three points in detail.

The bid/offer spread   It goes without saying that any market in which it is possible to trade has a price at which the offerer of the quote is prepared to buy and a higher one at which he is prepared to sell. The spread may only be one basis point in a highly liquid market, such as CME financial futures contracts or it may be five to ten basis points as in the case of spot US Dollar versus Sterling quotes. It is of course possible to get a 'choice price' i.e. where the bid and the offer are pitched at the same price. Such quotes would normally be crossed against each other with the buyer and seller satisfying each other's requirements to the extent of the lowest common denominator. If a cross does not occur, it is for one of two reasons, either the trade requirements are imbalanced e.g. a bid for one unit, but offered one hundred units, or alternatively, one counterparty cannot conclude the trade because it does not have credit lines for the other counterparty. Therefore, a switch of counterparty is required. Neither of these occurrences suggest a true market in the underlying commodity.

The size of trades and their frequency   Unless the size of the option portfolio which is being delta hedged in the cash market is substantial, i.e. tens of millions of Dollars, the individual trade sizes will be too small to allow efficient cash hedges to be undertaken. This point can be illustrated by examining the hedge ratio curve and comparing changes in spot prices with the change in the delta:

Figure 50

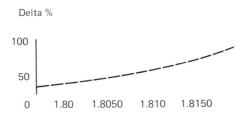

If the hedge ratio increases as above from 45% to 55% because spot has moved up from 1.80 to 1.8150 this will give rise to an increase in the hedge requirement of £100 000 for a call option on £1 mio. If this exercise were to be carried out at 25 basis point intervals it would require four trades of £25 000 face value. Alternatively, one hedge could be undertaken of £100 000 when the rate reached 1.8150. The problem with this approach is that you have a lag to market movements of 150 basis points which could potentially cost you USD 1,500 on this particular option. Can these expenses be absorbed by the daily erosion of the time value which you will receive? Neither of these alternatives provide an attractive practical solution for hedging the whole of an option portfolio in the cash and futures markets.

The rational behaviour of the foreign exchange markets   Operators in the foreign exchange markets will often argue that the market is as near as possible an example of a perfect market as can be achieved, a sentiment with which I would not take issue. However, there is room for discussion in this argument when applied to the theory of currency options. The first is that markets do not always behave in a rational manner, especially when the currency is trading at or near a 'CHART POINT'. That is to say there may be unfilled gaps in the market where bids or offers were not shown to the market. Prices may exhibit the following pattern:

23–28 Paid, 25–30 Paid   40   Bid without the offer

If rational behaviour were being exhibited, the price after 25–30 should be, say, 28–33, but if 40 bid without the offer is the next price, it indicates that demand exceeds supply albeit temporarily and therefore hedges are inaccessible between the last 30 offer and the next offer which has yet to be shown in the market. This raises the point that although the market is near perfect, i.e. a seller can almost always be found to satisfy a buyer (or vice versa), it may on occasions be at a price which is not adjacent to the last traded price.

Selling volatility

By selling options you are selling volatility and one of the assumptions of the formula is that volatility remains constant throughout the life of the option which may not be the case. As a general rule, if you sell volatility and delta hedge and it declines, you will make a profit because you will either be able to repurchase your short option position at a lower cost than that which you originally sold it for or, alternatively, you need to undertake less hedge transactions thereby incurring less foreign exchange dealing losses. If volatility increases, the converse is true with either replacement cost of the option increasing or foreign exchange dealing losses costing more than the daily time value which is received.

Black, Scholes and the European option

All the research carried out by Professors Black and Scholes related to European options and took no account of the ability of the option holder to require early exercise. This caused traders to price options which are likely to be exercised early on the spot value of the currency whilst those options which are not likely to be exercised early were priced on the outright forward value of the currency. The formula assumes a constant interest rate differential between the currencies and that hedges will gain the same forward cost or benefit throughout the life of the option, irrespective of when they are concluded. This is not the case as interest rate differentials do frequently change inter alia causing the forward points to deviate from those originally used and assumed in the formula.

The validity of the formula

It may seem from what has been said so far that the formula contains too many imponderables to make it a useable tool. This theory is not subscribed to here and I believe that there has been an element of misunderstanding about what Professor Black and Scholes were trying to achieve and what they were actually saying. The formula says that if the assumptions are valid and the implied volatility used in the formula is (*a*) correct and (*b*) constant, then cash flows similar to that which will arise from a currency option can be emulated. Perhaps this was taken to mean that if you sold currency options and delta hedged in the cash or futures markets, you would actually create an option. Both transactions would then have a neutralising effect on each other. The formula only gives a good approximation of the likely cost of hedging if the assumptions are correct and the various constituent factors which go to make up an option price trade consistent with the original projections.

By reducing the option to a manageable and easily recognisable factor, the delta, it is possible to hedge options written with options purchased, but not necessarily with the same strike price and maturity. An option cannot deviate far from its true value because the put call parity test will be applied by arbitrageurs and the mispriced option price will be quickly corrected. There is one minor exception to this argument, and that is if the sum of the bid offer spreads in the cash and the two options which make up the synthetic strategy is too great. If this occurs it will allow options to be mispriced to the extent of the spread before arbitrage can take place.

What of fat tails?

Fat tails is a term used to describe unexpected events in the value of the underlying which were statistically less likely to happen than the norm, and therefore, fall outside of the normal bell curve. To examine this phenomenon in more detail we first need to look at the use to which statistics and the bell curve are put.

As stated earlier historical volatility is calculated by taking day to day exchange rate changes and measuring the daily standard deviation. This information is then turned into a plot by using the lognormal distribution. A lognormal distribution is used rather than a normal distribution because of the bias towards infinity in exchange rate movements, that is to say, a currency can never have a negative worth but, mathematically, it can go to infinity. In practice, neither event is likely to occur but there is a mathematical bias towards infinity which changes the shape of the bell curve from normal to lognormal.

Figure 51

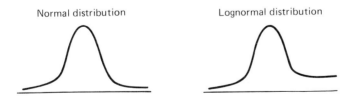

If one uses daily standard deviation as the measure of risk it can be split into three likely events.

1. STD equal to 68.3% probability
2. STD equal to 95.4% probability
3. STD equal to 99.7% probability

The problem which fat tails presents is in rehedging a portfolio with cash or futures when an unexpected occurrence will cause a movement in the underlying currency to widen the shape of the curve and require extra rehedging to be undertaken.

Curve A represents the original measure of volatility used in the pricing model whilst curve B is the increased volatility which is encountered in the market. If one were to ascribe percentage movements to these two values, it could be that curve A represents a $\frac{1}{2}$% per day movement whilst curve B represents a $\frac{3}{4}$% per day movement. This could make curve A equal to 10% p.a. volatility and curve B equal to 15% p.a. volatility which in turn would change the shape of the delta (hedge ratio) plot to a much shallower gradient, e.g.

Figure 52

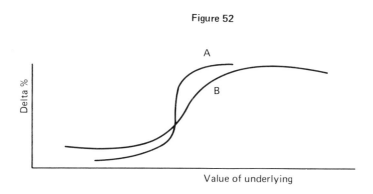

This phenomenon is not nearly so important in a portfolio of options which has been hedged with options unless the strike prices or maturity dates are significantly different. This is because the unexpected occurrence which gives rise to the fat tail will affect both positions in a similar way.

To return to the question of correctly modelling American options on currencies. What are the effects of the ability to exercise before maturity on the fair value and the hedge ratio? In the late 1970s Professors Cox, Ross and Rubinstein developed a method of pricing which is suitable for an option which is subject to early exercise. This method is known as binominal approximation (approximation is the term used not because it is particularly fallible but because it cannot be mathematically proved 100%.) A tree of possible spot market paths is produced and the value of the cash flows emanating from the cash (or futures) position is compared with the cash flows emanating from the option position. If the former is greater than the latter, the method assumes that the delta should correctly be 100%, the gamma 0% and that early exercise should arise e.g. see Figure 53.

Figure 53

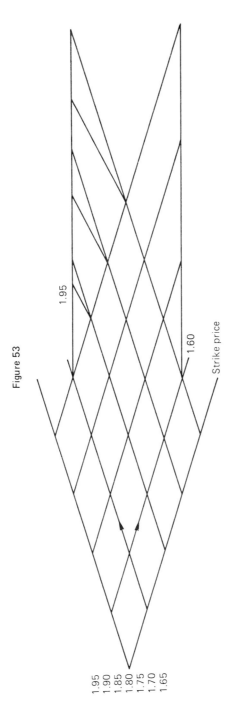

1.95

1.60

Strike price

1.95
1.90
1.85
1.80
1.75
1.70
1.65

Figure 53 shows a typical tree with each node representing the point at which the cash flows are assessed. The number of iterations in the life of the option is not defined but should be assumed to be constant, thus increasing the frequency of measurement of shorter dated options. The cash flows will continually be assessed until such a time when the future cash flow of the cash position exceeds that of the option, at which point early exercise will be triggered.

Early exercise of options on futures contracts is slightly different because the holder cannot gain forward points (or an interest rate differential) through exercising the option to acquire a position in the futures market. What he does acquire, however, if he exercises an option on a deep in the money futures contract is a substantial positive margin carry, which can be invested to yield a positive interest rate return, or alternatively, a position in the underlying futures whose positive margin can be used to offset negative margin calls on other contracts.

What is the rationale behind early exercise of options which are deep in the money? There is a basic assumption that the option contract is covering, or hedging, an equal and opposite position in the cash market and that this position has a known expiry date. The equal and opposite position can either be by way of a foreign exchange forward (or futures) position or, in the case of a corporate hedger, a known future transaction related exchange risk. Perhaps the simplest way of demonstrating the effect of a rationale behind early exercise is to consider the following example of a UK exporter who has purchased a Sterling call option to hedge a known US Dollar receipt which is due to be received in six months' time.

Day one (hedge established)

Current spot is USD/GBP 1.70. He purchases a 1.70 American style call option for six months in an amount of GBP 1 mio. (As a point of interest, the forward swap for the 6 month period is US cents 2.00. This is not relevant to the buyer of the option however.) The buyer has the following cash flows in six months' time.

Income Currency	Hedged by	Providing Income Sterling
USD 1 700 000	American call option at a strike of 1.70 for six months' duration.	£1 000 000

Day ninety (date of early exercise)

The prevailing spot rate of exchange has risen to USD/GBP 1.92 and on checking the delta and gamma on the option which he owns, he finds that the delta has risen to 100% and the gamma has fallen to 0% signifying that the movements in the option price are closely paralleling those of the spot USD/GBP rate. He then checks two further prices in the market. Firstly, the price of the option which is trading at 10 basis points either side of its intrinsic value (i.e. 1.92 minus 1.70 = 22.00. The quote he receives is US cents 21.90 to 22.10). Secondly, the forward swap points from today (day 90) to the maturity date of his option which is the same date as his receipt of US Dollars (day 180), the price being US cents 1.25 to 1.20.

Analysing this information, he draws the conclusion that the hedge has served its useful purpose and should be terminated because statistically using current data, specifically current volatility, there is little chance of the spot rate falling to the exercise price in the remaining three months' life of the option. He therefore has to decide if he wishes to sell the option and purchase forward Sterling to complete the transaction, or early exercise the option which he owns and swap the Sterling proceeds received in the forward market back to the date of receipt of his US Dollars. (This operation is to all intents and purposes the same as borrowing US Dollars to pay to the option writer and investing the Sterling proceeds on deposit.)

Example (a) Sell option purchase forward Sterling

Sell option received	cents	21.90 +
Original strike price of option	cents	170.00 +
Current fwd rate USD/GBP		190.80 −
Points gained if this method is undertaken	(cents)	1.10

Example (b) Exercise option early and swap Sterling

Sell spot Sterling	192.00 −
Purchase fwd Sterling	190.80 +
Points gained if this method is undertaken (cents)	1.20

It can clearly be demonstrated from the above examples that call options on high interest rate currencies with a delta of 100% which are not exercised prior to maturity will give rise to a real loss not just an opportunity cost. The choice for a corporate hedger between early exercise and sell option buy forward methods, is not as clear cut as it is for a financial institution options trader in that the corporate hedger may be constrained by margins, use of facilities etc. There is no question of what should happen in the case of a financial institution option trader. If he is long of a call option on a high interest rate currency where the delta is 100% and the gamma is 0%, he should exercise his right to take delivery of the high interest rate currency as soon as possible. The only general exception to this rule is if the exercise or assignment costs outweigh the forward points to be gained. If the option owned is hedging an option sold where both deltas are at 100% it is safer to exercise early and swap the proceeds on a day to day basis because in theory you should be receiving at any time an exercise notice for the option which you have sold. If the option owned is hedging a short Sterling position in the foreign exchange market, the Sterling received as a result of early exercise should be swapped to the maturity date of that position. This argument still holds even if the short position is being swapped day to day because you still have a daily carry cost for the short position which can be eliminated by early exercise.

There is one possible situation when early exercise could give rise to a loss, that is if you exercise a short dated option and a very large movement takes place in the value of the underlying currency. This could happen because the delta at 100% is indicating that at current volatility you will be exercised in the short option. However, in extreme cases like 'Black Friday', when the Dollar/Mark movement was of the order of 5% in one trading session, normal rules obviously do not apply.

Chapter 8

Portfolio Analysis

It can be seen that tracking the profit or loss of one option position through time and with movements in the value of the underlying currency, volatility and interest rate differentials can be difficult enough but imagine multiplying this degree of difficulty by twenty different option positions, some puts, some calls, most with different strike prices and maturity dates and adding a position in the underlying currency as well. Without a computer model it is virtually impossible to achieve. In the early days of options traders turned to computer systems which calculated their open positions in delta equivalent terms as the first step to portfolio analysis. Since then, the systems and the traders have become ever more sophisticated and measure portfolios in terms of deltas, gammas, thetas and vegas. This chapter is limited to the factors which deal in essence with the problems inherent in an option portfolio. They are delta, gamma and profitability.

DELTA (HEDGE RATIO)

The delta of an option is the rate of change of the option value relative to the rate of change in the value of the underlying currency. This figure is not constant and changes with rises or falls in the value of the underlying currency, time erosion, volatility and interest rate differential changes. An option may start with a delta of 50% but at maturity it *must* end with either a delta of 100% or 0% because at maturity it *must* either be exercised (100%) and is moving directly parallel with the value of the underlying currency, or will expire worthless (0%) and therefore have no direct relationship (no statistical chance of being exercised) with the underlying currency.

Delta is a useful tool in that it condenses all of the various options in a portfolio into a manageable single unit, i.e. the equivalent value in the underlying currency. Consider the following simple option portfolio of one option and a position in the underlying currency:

Day 1 with spot at 1.80

Sold Call £1 million   Strike 1.80 1 mth Delta 50% = Short £500 000
Bought £0.5 million Spot 1.80   Delta 100% = Long £500 000

Nett position in underlying   NIL

By doing this you have sold one problem, i.e. brought the values back to a position in the underlying currency which today is a nil position. The problem that you have created is that your delta positions will not be the same tomorrow (or indeed through the life of the portfolio) firstly, because of changes in the value of the underlying currency, changes in volatility, changes in interest rate differentials and changes in time to maturity of the instruments. Secondly, parts of the portfolio will mature at different times leaving you mismatches.

Day 12 with spot at 1.78

Sold Call £1 million Strike 1.80 Originally 1 month

	New Delta 35% =	Short £350 000
Bought £0.5 million spot @ 1.80 Delta Still 100%		
	=	Long £500 000
Nett position in underlying on day 12 of portfolio		Long £150 000

In the chapter which deals with the assumptions of the formula it was clear that to replicate an option with positions in the underlying currency each individual movement in the delta equivalent position needs to be hedged as it happens. This is not possible because of bid/offer spreads and the small size of the hedges required.

Problems inherent in the above portfolio and effects on the profit and loss account

The first problem which arises is that the delta equivalent position is now £150 000 long (overbought) and the option has moved out of the money. This means that you need to decide whether you still need the £150 000 long position to hedge the option or if it is surplus to requirements. Also, because the option which you have granted has moved out of the money, it is only moving at 35% of the rate of change of the underlying currency now and not at 50% which was the rate of change at the time of grant. It is usual in a short option portfolio if it is being run for profit to try and achieve a delta neutral position and therefore the £150 000 would be sold off to achieve this end. (It is probable that some action would have been taken between the day of grant and day 12, therefore the delta would not have moved from 50% to 35% in one movement, except in the case of very short dated options.) This highlights the second problem which will be caused. With a short option portfolio all hedges in the underlying currency incur exchange losses for the writer and the income is limited to the original premium received. If you are fortunate and have priced the option on a higher annualised volatility than that which actually occurs, you should be left with a modest profit after rehedging the option granted. If, however, the option granted needs more hedging than was originally anticipated, because volatility in the underlying currency is greater than that which is charged, you will incur a loss.

Consider the positions in the underlying currency from the above examples assuming that you seek delta neutrality and on day 12 you sell the surplus £150 000 position in the spot market and revalue the balance.

Day of grant	purchased	GBP 500 000 @ 1.80 =	USD 900 000
Day 12	retain	GBP 350 000 @ 1.78 =	USD 623 000
Day 12	sell	GBP 150 000 @ 1.78 =	USD 267 000
		Loss of	USD 10 000

If this loss of USD 10 000 is covered by a depreciation in the value of the option you have not yet realised your loss because you could repurchase the option sold and at the same time resell the underlying currency purchased, thus making a nominal profit or loss on the two trades. For this reason, when trading an option portfolio it is important to 'mark to market' and account for profits and losses on a daily basis (this relates mainly to banks and other professional market makers) rather than wait until maturity and then account. This will help you to avoid nasty shocks when you realise that you received Y for granting an option and lost Y × 2 by hedging positions in the underlying currency.

Looking at this example in another way, if the purchased £150 000 is surplus to requirement and is sold in the spot markets you have incurred a loss to the extent of:

£150 000	@	1.80	=	USD 270 000
£150 000	@	1.78	=	USD 267 000
				USD 3 000

If you originally received USD 12 000 in premium for granting the option you can only incur the rehedging losses four times during the life of the option. Do not forget that the delta at maturity must be either 0% or 100% and you therefore need to either own GBP 1 million if exercised or GBP nil if not exercised. Figure 2 in Chapter 3 (page 18) is a diagram of delta movements over a range of values for the underlying currency and from this it can be seen how the delta is likely to react.

Portfolio analysis will also show how your profit and loss will be affected from today until tomorrow by changes in the value of the underlying currency.

GAMMA

Delta is the first derivative of the spot price, gamma is the second, being the volatility of the delta of an option. This phenomenon is best illustrated by looking at the movements in the underlying currency for an option with different maturity dates.

This example relates to two options which were at the money when granted. One is for a one month period and the other for a three month period. The value of the underlying currency at the date of grant is 1.80. See Figure 54.

Figure 54

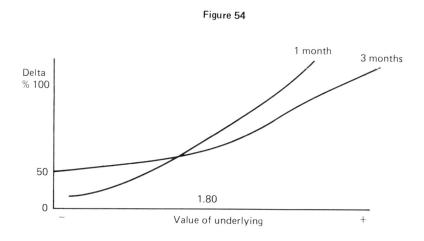

It can be seen that the movement of the delta of the one month option is more pronounced than that of the three month option and they are equal at only one point in time (disregarding maturity when both must have a delta of 0% or 100%). The point at which the deltas are the same is when the value of the underlying currency and the strike price is the same and statistically both options have a 50% chance of being exercised. (For the sake of this example, the effects of interest rate differentials have been ignored but do not forget that with American options on high interest rate currencies the call is priced on the spot price of the underlying currency, thus an 'at the money option' is where spot and strike are the same.) Puts are priced on the outright forward price of the underlying currency. Thus an 'at the money' option is where the outright forward and the strike are the same e.g.

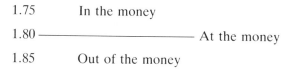

1.75   In the money

1.80 ——————————————————— At the money

1.85   Out of the money

Puts on GBP vs USD with spot at 1.80 and outright forward at 1.78

1.75   Out of the money

1.78 ————————————————— At the money

1.80   In the money

1.85

Another point to remember is that because of this situation the sum of the delta of the put and the delta of the call of an American option with the same strike price can during the life of an option equal more than 100%, but not at maturity, where only the put or the call will be exercised and therefore the sum of the deltas can only be 100%.

There are a number of ways to look at gamma. The two most popular methods are gammas as a change in the delta and in portfolio terms gamma negative or gamma positive.

Gamma as a percentage change in the delta

The traditional definition of gamma is the rate of change of the delta for one point (i.e. 100 basis point change) in the underlying.

Not all option deltas change at the same rate in response to a one point change in the underlying. The rate of change of the delta is a function of time, volatility and the strike price of the option. It is necessary to know how a particular option, or portfolio of options, will react to movements in the underlying to ensure that the correct delta hedges are concluded. This can be illustrated by reference to an at-the-money option which starts with a delta of 50%. Rises in the value of the underlying will cause the delta to increase about 50%, whilst falls in the value of the underlying will cause the delta to decrease below 50%. The increases and decreases in the delta as a result of increases and decreases in the underlying are not linear but dynamic.

Figures 55 and 56 (pages 144 and 145) show the effect on deltas of various options as a result of changes in the underlying currency, time to maturity and implied volatility.

It can be seen from the diagrams that three factors influence the shape of the delta curve, namely, time to maturity of the option, the extent to which the option is in or out-of-the-money and implied volatility. What influence do these individual factors have?

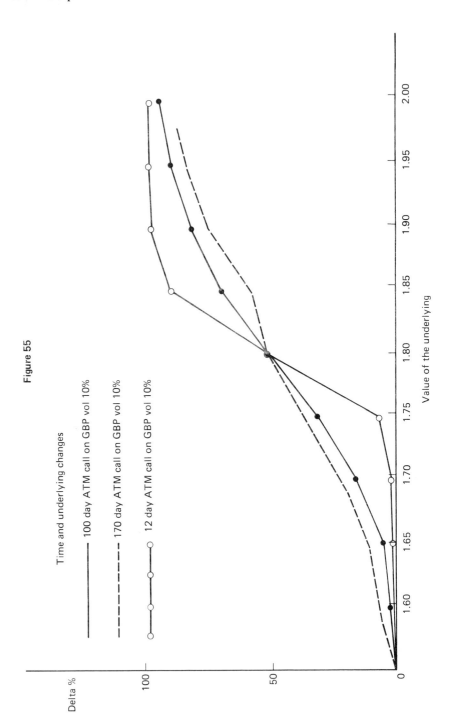

Figure 55

Time and underlying changes

———— 100 day ATM call on GBP vol 10%

‑ ‑ ‑ ‑ 170 day ATM call on GBP vol 10%

—o— 12 day ATM call on GBP vol 10%

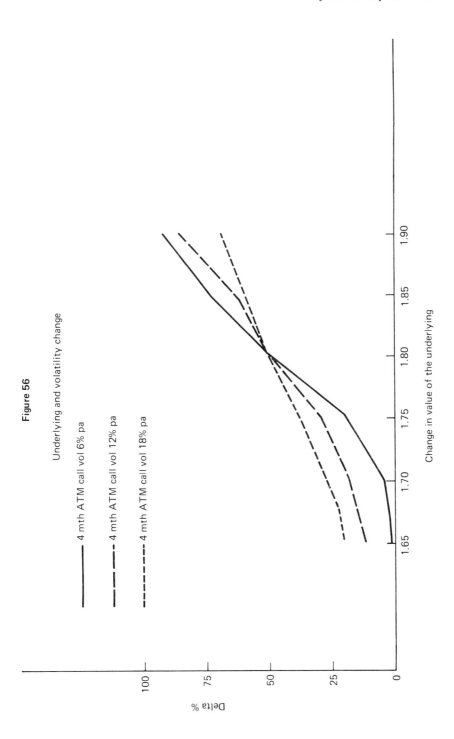

Figure 56

Underlying and volatility change

—— 4 mth ATM call vol 6% pa

– – – 4 mth ATM call vol 12% pa

- - - - 4 mth ATM call vol 18% pa

Delta %

100
75
50
25
0

1.65 1.70 1.75 1.80 1.85 1.90

Change in value of the underlying

Time to maturity

As a general rule, shorter dated options which are deep in or out-of-the-money tend towards a low gamma, i.e. the delta does not change that dramatically for a point move in the underlying. If the delta of the 12 day option in Figure 55 is split into three parts it will be seen that the area at-the-money is much more susceptible to changes in the underlying.

Change in underlying		*Change in delta*	
From	*To*	*From*	*To*
1.65	1.75	0%	7.6%
1.75	1.85	7.6%	91.8%
1.85	1.95	91.8%	99.7%

Undertaking the same comparison with the 100 day to maturity option, a smoother pattern is observed.

Change in underlying		*Change in delta*	
From	*To*	*From*	*To*
1.65	1.75	5.4%	30.2%
1.75	1.85	30.2%	68.9%
1.85	1.95	68.9%	91.4%

Whilst the effect on the delta of the 170 day to maturity option is even smoother still.

Change in underlying		*Change in delta*	
From	*To*	*From*	*To*
1.65	1.75	12.4%	35.1%
1.75	1.85	35.1%	62.8%
1.85	1.95	62.8%	82.8%

The gamma of an option measures how much the option delta will move for a one point move in the underlying.

Figure 57 (page 147) illustrates how the delta on the three options have changed for a five point move up in the value of the underlying.

Figure 57

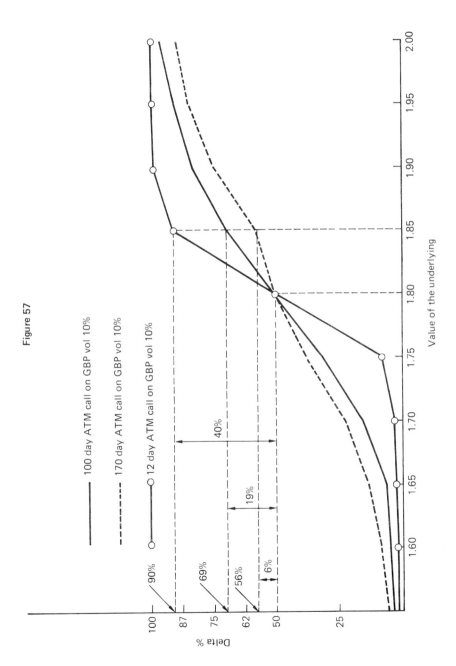

Options	*Change in delta*	*Gamma*
170 day option	50% to 56%	$\dfrac{6\%}{5} = 1.2\%$
100 day option	50% to 69%	$\dfrac{19\%}{5} = 3.8\%$
12 day option	50% to 90%	$\dfrac{40\%}{5} = 8.0\%$

It can be deduced from Figure 57 that ATM short dated options have high gammas whilst their deep in and deep out-of-the-money counterparts have low gammas. Reference to the time print outs in Chapter 3 will show that gamma and theta demonstrate the same properties in this respect. The following examination of a short dated option will show that this type of option has a high gamma and theta at-the-money but declining as the option moves in or out-of-the-money.

Type of Options	*Delta/Gamma/Theta*	*Reason*
Deep (10 cents) in the money one month option	95%/1.6%/.01 basis point	The premium consists of almost all intrinsic value. It is acting almost identically like a position in the underlying currency. Almost no time and volume content (extrinsic) value to write off.
At-the-money one month option	50%/6.8%/4 basis points	At-the-money options are the most expensive in terms of extrinsic value. The premium consists entirely of time and volatility costs which,in the event of no move in the underlying, will need to be eroded to zero by maturity.
Deep (10 cents) out of-the-money option	4.2%/1.5%/0.009 basis point	An out-of-the-money option has a very low cost which suggests a very low probability of exercise at maturity if

the estimate of volatil-
ity is correct. A one
point move in the un-
derlying is not greatly
going to increase or
decrease the probabil-
ity of option maturity
in the money.

Figure 58 (page 150) shows the gamma of options with various maturities and with various strike prices. It is clear that the shorter an option duration and the nearer it is to being at-the-money, the more susceptible it is to changes in the value of the underlying currency.

Position from today until maturity

Running an analysis from today until tomorrow is necessary because it will tell you what will happen to your portfolio overnight. It is also important to know how well hedged you are in the future. To reiterate again, the only option portfolio which does not require some ongoing attention is one which is matched as to maturity date and strike, since even the smallest mismatches, which at inception seem harmless, can cause problems at maturity and will almost certainly not be highlighted by the model, at least not in the early days of the option life. An example of this is again where spot and strike coincide at maturity and, say, you have purchased an OTC option which expires at 3pm London time to cover an exchange listed option which expires later in the afternoon New York time. You could conceivably have three or four hours of no cover which could give rise to losses if you are not able to hedge successfully. It may seem at this point that no mismatches in positions are being advocated. This is not the case as you are unlikely to make a profit if you run a totally square book. It is, however, very important that you understand the risks that you are running and the consequences. Probably the best way to trade a portfolio is by trading volatility both implied and historical or a mixture of both if you believe one is out of line but setting your limits for delta, gamma and profit and loss at realistic levels for your institution. If you get the chance to repurchase cheaply an option which you have sold think twice before you pass up the chance.

Another discipline which is worth adopting is regularly to familiarise yourself with the shape of the volatility curve through the various listed option periods. Implied volatility for the various periods in the listed option markets will vary and patterns can emerge from time to time. It is worth knowing how implied volatility normally reacts as an option approaches maturity, e.g. quite often the spot month is sold off in the run up to maturity.

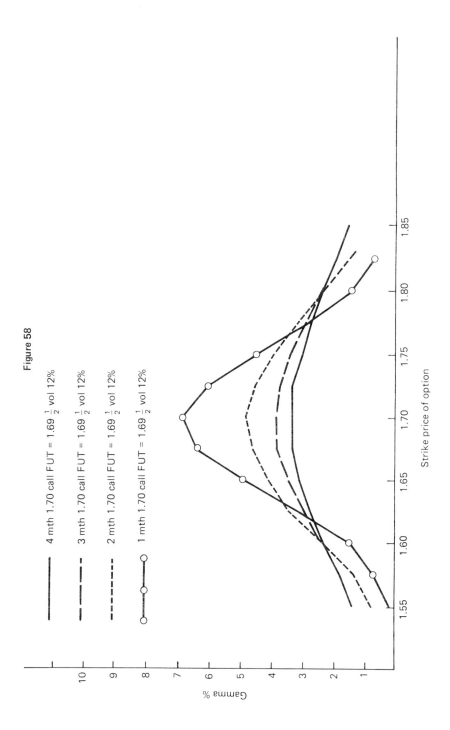

Figure 58

4 mth 1.70 call FUT = 1.69 $\frac{1}{2}$ vol 12%

3 mth 1.70 call FUT = 1.69 $\frac{1}{2}$ vol 12%

2 mth 1.70 call FUT = 1.69 $\frac{1}{2}$ vol 12%

1 mth 1.70 call FUT = 1.69 $\frac{1}{2}$ vol 12%

This chapter deals with a portfolio of options and not a simple hedge or trading one option for gain and therefore it is necessary to look at the overall picture. The various choices when hedging a portfolio are too numerous to detail but the four most important factors to consider are:

1. Is the portfolio delta neutral and gamma negative today and if so what are the assumptions that you are making?
2. Is the portfolio delta neutral and gamma positive today and if so what are the assumptions that you are making?
3. Position from today until tomorrow with regard to potential P + L.
4. Position from today until the maturity of the portfolio with regard to P + L.

In the introduction to this chapter it said that there are three basic areas to consider – delta, gamma, and profitability.

Delta neutral and gamma negative

A portfolio can be delta neutral but still be gamma negative by your having written more options (in delta terms) than you have purchased and therefore all hedges which are undertaken in the foreign exchange markets will give rise to losses. This position will normally be reflected in a daily accrual of premium in your favour because you should be receiving time value. However, do not forget that you have sold volatility and therefore if volatility is greater than the rate at which you sold it, you will incur a greater loss in hedging and rehedging than the premium accruing to you.

If you have only sold options without purchasing any back to cover your position, your daily accrual of premium will be substantial, but if you run into a period of very high volatility in the foreign exchange markets you will be 'hurt' in two ways. Firstly, your rehedging costs in the form of exchange losses will be very high and, secondly, if at this stage you choose to purchase some options to protect the portfolio you will be charged a higher volatility than that which you have sold. Therefore, you will be locking in losses.

If you choose to run a portfolio delta neutral and gamma negative, you are making the assumption that the future volatility in the foreign exchange markets will be less than that which is reflected in the current price of options.

Another area to watch is options with a maturity of less than twenty days which can act almost like spot foreign exchange positions with a minimal premium for the writer to protect himself. The most exaggerated case of this type is the option with one day to maturity and with the spot and strike price at the same level.

Spot Rate	Delta Equiv Posn	Spot Rate	Delta Equiv Posn
1.7850	+ £ 90 000	1.8025	+ £590 000
1.7875	+ £130 000	1.8050	+ £580 000
1.7900	+ £180 000	1.8075	+ £750 000
1.7925	+ £250 000	1.8100	+ £820 000
1.7950	+ £320 000	1.8125	+ £870 000
1.7975	+ £410 000	1.8150	+ £910 000
1.8000	+ £500 000		

It can be seen from this example that careful hedging is required because not only will you have the overnight risk to bear from today until tomorrow where hedging may not be possible, but you will also have a worse delta position on the day the option matures, i.e.

```
0% hedge                                          100% hedge

1.75 ——————————————— 1.7999/1.8001 ——————————————— 1.85
```

You can imagine what happens if you have a maturing option on your books where the spot and strike price coincide and you only have a modest premium left to protect yourself. Every time spot moves about the strike price you have to make a value judgement. Is spot going to stay above strike and therefore do you purchase the balance of Sterling to cover exercise? The converse is also true if spot falls below strike. Do you sell off the remaining holding in Sterling as you do not expect to be exercised? In both cases, what happens if I am wrong? The answer is that you end up buying back your original position in the underlying currency at a loss!

A simple rule to remember for a delta neutral and a gamma negative portfolio is that the hedges which you are forced to undertake will give rise to losses and your premium income to offset against these losses is limited where your hedging costs are not.

Now let us look at ways in which gamma can be used in a portfolio of options.

Delta Neutral Gamma Negative

1.83 Even Greater Loss	Exchange losses incurred if no
1.82 Greater Loss	rehedging is undertaken
1.81 Loss	

Current spot 1.80 Profit ————————————————————Time Value Earned

1.79 Loss	Exchange losses incurred if no
1.78 Greater Loss	rehedging is undertaken
1.77 Even Greater Loss	

As can be seen from this example, the profits accrued at the current spot level out and losses start to accrue the further the spot moves away. The extent of the profit and loss depends on the degree of the gamma negativity of the portfolio and in fact it could read as profits at 1.81 and 1.79 in a more defensive portfolio but the concept is correct. You could try to neutralise the rehedging losses by anticipating moves in the value of the underlying currency and being overlong or overshort in the foreign exchange market. This does not, however, accord with delta neutrality. A further word on revaluing of portfolios is called for here. It is worthwhile revaluing the portfolio at current values of volatility, spot and relative interest rates on a daily basis because this is actually what you have to control in your positions. If you start to make assumptions about future values of the underlying currencies, volatility, relative interest rates and whether or not you will be exercised on particular options, you are not being true to the concept of running a portfolio. In summary, it is valid to revalue a portfolio daily on current values and take profit or loss on valuation to the P + L account. One further ancillary point—if you own call options on high interest rate currencies which are so far in money that the hedge ratio is 100% (or almost) and you have a corresponding short position in the underlying currency which is causing you a negative swap cost, it is worth early exercising this option and utilising the proceeds to neutralise the cost of carry of the foreign exchange position.

Delta neutral and gamma positive

A portfolio can be delta neutral and gamma positive by your having purchased more options (in delta terms) than you have written and therefore all hedges undertaken in the foreign exchange markets will yield you a profit to offset your daily cost which is the erosion of time value of the options which you own.

There are a number of ways in which a portfolio can be structured to be delta neutral. This strategy is usually undertaken when there is a high level of intra day volatility in the markets which will allow the owner of the option to undertake sufficient hedges in the underlying currency to yield more foreign exchange dealing profits than the daily cost (theta) of owning the option. It should be noted that the daily cost of owning accelerates towards the expiry of the option. The assumption that you are making by undertaking this strategy is that there will be a high level of volatility within the foreign exchange markets and if volatility decreases or is in fact minimal, you will not receive sufficient foreign exchange dealing profits to offset your cost of owning the option. However, your loss is limited to the amount of premium paid for the original option positions.

Delta Neutral Gamma Positive

1.83 Even Greater Profit	Profit earned over cost of time
1.82 Greater Profit	value if portfolio is rehedged at
1.81 Profit	this level

Current spot 1.80 Loss ————————————————Time Value Paid

1.79 Profit	Profit earned over cost of time
1.78 Greater Profit	value if portfolio is rehedged at
1.77 Even Greater Profit	this level

As can be seen from this example, the loss accrued if the value of the underlying currency changes little or not at all from today until tomorrow. This is because you have purchased more options than you have written and therefore the erosion of time value is working against you. This can be particularly pronounced with options maturing tomorrow and having strike prices at the money. These options can lose as much as $\frac{1}{2}$% flat of the fact value overnight i.e. $5 000 per $1 million and you should therefore at least be aware of the consequences if spot does not move. However, this type of position is an option buyer's 'dream' if you are long on option at the money with only one day to run and the spot and strike correspond and the spot moves backwards and forwards through the strike price because the delta can be ignored or more realistically on the day of maturity regarded as 0% or 100% thus enabling you to go in and out of the foreign exchange market as spot moves back and forth through the strike.

Another method of maintaining a delta neutral and gamma positive portfolio is to purchase at or in the money options to hedge out of the money options written. This is normally done to original delta neutrality and you will normally have a deficit of premium which will have to be funded from the profit realised on hedges undertaken in the foreign exchange market. Again do not forget that low volatility means fewer hedges and therefore you may not cover your premium deficit incurred by purchasing more expensive options than those which you have written.

A third way of maintaining a delta neutral and gamma positive strategy is by purchasing a shorter dated option than those which have been written, e.g. by purchasing a one month 1.80 call option to hedge a three month 1.80 call written. The hedge ratio of the one month option should move faster than that of a three month option. Therefore, all hedges undertaken in the foreign exchange markets should yield you a profit. This should only be undertaken when a short period of volatility in the foreign exchange market is expected followed by a period of relative calm. By undertaking this strategy you are left unhedged after expiration of the original one month option purchased and need then to recover either by purchasing another one month option or repurchasing the two month option sold. This will obviously have to be concluded at the current level of volatility. Check it on your model to see what the effects are but remember that options have a yield curve which will not necessarily be flat, i.e.

One month Fairvalue	Two month Fairvalue	Three month Fairvalue
3.05	4.15	5.00

It is worth checking what happens if the option moves either deeply 'in' or 'out' of the money.

Position from today until tomorrow

The third measure of option portfolio risk is what will happen to the portfolio from today until tomorrow over a range of spot prices. This relates to a common sense approach and the amount of losses you are prepared to bear to support your view of what will happen in the markets. Do not forget that unless you have purchased and sold exactly the same option (a matched portfolio) you are running a risk of profit or loss. In addition to changes in the spot rate, changes in relative interest rates and changes in volatility will also affect the profit and loss profile and it is worth revaluing the portfolio over a range of volatilities and forward rates to see the effect.

Glossary of Terminology

Abandon—To allow an option to expire without exercising it.

American option—An option that may be exercised at any time up to the expiration time for delivery to take place two business days after the exercise date.

At the money—The underlying currency price stands at (or very close to) the exercise price.

Call option—A call option contract confers the right to buy a fixed amount of currency (usually in exchange for US Dollars) within a predetermined period of time.

Cash settlement option—This is an option where the seller grants the buyer the option but physical settlement does not take place. The holder receives the difference between spot and strike if the option is exercised.

Certificateless trading—Options are a form of certificateless trading with the evidence of ownership being found in the brokers' or banks' books and the client's contract note.

Closing purchase transaction—A transaction in which a writer (seller) buys back an option identical to one which he has written, thus extinguishing his liability as a writer.

Closing sale transaction—A transaction in which the holder of an option disposes of it in the market to another buyer.

Contract—An option issued by the writer.

Counter currency—The currency to be exchanged for the underlying currency.

Cover—Underlying currency pledged as collateral to the clearing authority for a written option.

Covered writer—The writer of a call option who pledges to the clearing authority the underlying currency.

Covered—The writer holds all the underlying currency for the option writer.

European option—An option which may be exercised at any time but delivery may only take place at maturity of the option.

Exercise date—The date on which the grantor accepts a notice of exercise.

Exercise notice—A formal notification to the clearing body or bank that the holder of an option wishes to exercise it by buying or selling the underlying currency.

Exercise price strike price—The exchange rate at which the option is granted and may be exercised in order to take delivery/deliver the underlying currency.

Expiration date—The latest date on which the grantor of an option will accept notice or exercise.

Expiration time—The latest time at which the grantor of an option will accept notice of exercise.

First settlement date—The first date on which the holder of an American option can effect delivery of the underlying currency against payment of the counter currency.

Grantor—The party that grants the option.

Holder—The purchaser or, if the purchaser subsequently assigns the option to another party, that party or any other subsequent holder in due course.

In-the-money-option—A call option whose exercise price is below the current market price of the underlying currency, or a put option whose exercise price is above the current market price of the underlying currency.

Intrinsic value—A call option has intrinsic value if the exercise price of the option is lower than the price of the underlying currency. A put option has intrinsic value if the exercise price of the option is higher than the price of the underlying currency. In each case, the intrinsic value is the difference between the exercise price and the price of the underlying currency.

Margin—The sum required as collateral from writers of options who are not covered by the lodgement of the underlying currency.

Net settlement amount—The amount payable to the holder on exercise of a cash settlement option.

Open interest—The number of option contracts outstanding at any one time.

Option—The right but not the obligation for the purchaser to exchange one predetermined amount of currency for another predetermined amount of currency at a specified rate on one specific date or between two specified dates as determined by the option contract.

Out-of-the-money-option—A call option whose exercise price is above the current price of the underlying currency or a put option whose exercise price is below the current price of the underlying currency.

Premium—The price paid by the buyer of an option to the seller of an option for a particular option.

Premium payment date—The date on which the premium is due.

Purchaser—The party that purchases the option.

Put option—A put option contract confers the right to sell a fixed amount of currency (usually in exchange for US dollars) within a predetermined period of time.

Regulatory body—Usually a 'Clearing House' which guarantees the integrity of the contract by receiving either collateral or cash from the option writer sufficient to discharge his obligations under his open contracts position.

Settlement date—(1) an American option, the second business day which immediately follows the exercise date of such option; (2) a European option, the second business day which immediately follows the expiration date of such option.

Spread—A purchase and sale of different series of options in the same class by the same principal.

Spread margin—The margin required for an open uncovered sale which is offset by an opening purchase of contracts of a different series in the same class by the same principal.

Time value—That part of the option premium which reflects the remaining life of an option. The longer the time remaining before expiry, the higher the time value will tend to be. (Refer to 'Intrinsic Value' which, added to 'Time Value', should be the premium.)

Traded option—An option which has an inherent value and may be sold as opposed to exercised as a method of releasing any intrinsic value. This differs from a traditional option which may normally only be exercised at maturity and for which no recognised secondary market exists.

Uncovered writer—A writer who does not own the underlying currency upon which the option is sold. Also referred to as a 'naked writer'.

Underlying currency—The currency in respect of which an option contract has been bought or sold (written).

Unit of trading or contract—The number of units of the underlying currency designated by the regulatory body as the subject of a single option contract e.g. a Chicago Mercantile Exchange US Dollar vs Pound Sterling contract is quoted as £62 500 being a single option.

Writer—The seller of an option contract.

Inland Revenue Statement of Practice

The Inland Revenue have been discussing with the London International Financial Futures Exchange the tax treatment of transactions in financial futures and options by investment trusts, unit trusts, pension funds and other non-trading companies. These discussions have resulted in the preparation of guidelines which have been the subject of consultations with other interested parties and are today being issued by the Inland Revenue in the form of the accompanying Statement of Practice.

SP 4/88   22 July 1988

TAX TREATMENT OF TRANSACTIONS IN FINANCIAL FUTURES AND OPTIONS

1. This Statement sets out the Inland Revenue's views on the tax treatment of transactions in financial futures and options carried out by investment trusts, unit trusts, pension funds, charities, and companies which either do not trade or whose principal trade is outside the financial area. The principles set out apply to all futures and options, whether traded on an exchange or otherwise.

2. Section 72 Finance Act 1985 provides, broadly, that transactions in commodity and financial futures and traded options on recognised exchanges will be treated as capital in nature unless they are regarded as profits or losses of a trade. Section 81 Finance Act 1987 extends this treatment to other transactions in futures and options. If, under normal statutory and case law principles, profits or losses fall to be treated as trading in nature then Sections 72 and 81 have no application to those profits or losses. It is therefore necessary first to determine whether or not a taxpayer is trading in futures or options without reference to the provisions of Sections 72 and 81.

3. Whether or not a taxpayer is trading is a question of fact to be determined by reference to all the facts and circumstances of the particular case. Consideration is given to the "badges of trade". Generally a person will not be regarded as trading if the transactions are infrequent or to hedge specific capital investments. An individual is unlikely to be regarded as trading as a result of purely speculative transactions in options or futures.

4.   If the taxpayer in question is a company, which would include an investment trust or authorised unit trust, it is necessary to consider not only the normal case law defining trading but also the case of Lewis Emanuel and Son Ltd v White (42 TC 369). The broad effect of the judgement in this case is that generally a company cannot speculate and that any transactions carried out by a company must either be trading or capital in nature.

5.   If a transaction in financial futures or options is clearly related to an underlying asset or transaction, then the tax treatment of the futures or options contract will follow that of the underlying asset or transaction. In general, the Inland Revenue take the view that this relationship exists where a futures or options contract is entered into in order to hedge an underlying transaction, asset or portfolio by reducing the risk relating to it; and the intention of the taxpayer in entering into the transaction is of considerable importance. Where the underlying transaction is itself treated as giving rise to a capital gain or loss, the related futures or options contract will also be treated as a capital matter and not as trading.

6.   The basic conditions which have to be met if the transaction is to be treated as hedging in this sense are:

> (1) the transaction must be economically appropriate to the reduction in risk of the underlying transaction, asset or portfolio; and
> (2) the price fluctuations of the options and futures must be directly and demonstrably related to the fluctuations in value or composition of the underlying transaction, asset or portfolio at the time the hedging transaction is initiated.

7.   This applies equally to long and short positions, and is not dependent upon the form of the eventual disposition of the position. In other words it will apply whether the futures position is closed out or held to maturity, or in the case of an options position, closed out, exercised or held to final expiry.

Examples

8.   Transactions would be treated as giving rise to capital gains or losses in the following circumstances:

> (1) A taxpayer who holds gilts sells gilt futures to protect the value of his capital in the event of a fall in the value of gilt-edged securities generally.
> (2) A taxpayer purchases an asset in two stages by purchasing a foreign currency future in advance of the purchase of an asset denominated in that currency, or by purchasing an option in respect of an underlying asset as a first step towards the acquisition of the asset itself.
> (3) A taxpayer who holds a broadly based portfolio sells index futures or purchases index put options to protect himself against

the risk to the value of the portfolio from a fall in the market, (provided the fall in the index futures or options is directly and demonstrably correlated to the loss on the portfolio as it was constituted at the date the hedge was initiated).

9. But even if a transaction is not a hedging transaction in the sense of paragraph 6 above, it may, nevertheless, be regarded as capital in nature, depending on all the facts and circumstances. To take two specific examples –

(1) If a taxpayer is committed to making a bond issue in the near future and enters into an interest rate future or option with a view to protecting himself against rises in interest costs before he is able to make the issue, the Revenue will regard the transaction as being of a capital nature.

(2) If a taxpayer sells or buys options or futures as an incidental and temporary part of a change in investment strategy, (e.g., changing the ratio of gilts and equities), that transaction is likely to be treated as being of a capital nature, if the transaction in the assets themselves would be a capital matter.

10. A further uncertainty may arise if a transaction is originally undertaken as a capital hedge but the underlying transaction or motive falls away. If the futures or options transaction is closed out within a reasonably short period after the underlying motive falls away then the transaction will continue to be treated as capital in nature in accordance with the principles outlined above. If however the transaction is not closed out at that time it may be arguable that any profit or loss arising subsequently is of a trading nature. In practice the Revenue would not normally take this point in view of the original intentions of the taxpayer and the practical difficulties of making the necessary calculation.

11. Where a company enters into these transactions as incidental to its trading activity, for example a manufacturer entering into transactions to hedge the price of his raw materials, then the profits or losses from these transactions would be taken into acount as part of the profits and losses of the trade.

International Exchanges

This appendix contains standard contract specifications for exchanges that provide services for foreign currency options.

CHICAGO MERCANTILE EXCHANGE
OPTION CONTRACT SPECIFICATIONS & MINIMUM MARGIN REQUIREMENTS

Option/Size	Hours	Months	Codes Clr/Tick	Min Fluctuation in Price	Limit	Last Day of Trading	Strike Price Intervals	Strategy-based Min. Margins for Naked Short positions	SPAN
Australian $ Options-One AD Futures Contract	7:20 2:00 (2:00)	Mar Jun Sep Dec & Serial Month Options	AD KA Calls JA Puts	.0001 = 1 pt. ($10.00/pt) ($10.00) cab = $5.00	Option ceases trading when corresponding future locks limit	2nd Friday prior to 3rd Wed of contract mo.	$/AD $.01 intervals e.g. $.70, $.71	Premium + $400	Refer to Daily SPAN risk arrays generated by the CME.
British Pound Options-One BP Futures Contract (62,500 BP)	7:20 2:00 (2:00)	Mar Jun Sep Dec & Serial Month Options	BP CP Calls PP Puts	.0002 = 2 pts. ($6.25/pt) ($12.50) cab = $6.25	Option ceases trading when corresponding future locks limit	2nd Friday prior to 3rd Wed of contract mo.	$/BP $.025 intervals e.g. $1.450, $1.475	Premium + $400	Refer to Daily SPAN risk arrays generated by the CME.
Canadian $ Options-One CD Futures Contract	7:20 2:00 (2:00)	Mar Jun Sep Dec & Serial Month Options	C1 CV Calls PV Puts	.0001 = 1 pt. ($10.00/pt) ($10.00) cab = $5.00	Option ceases trading when corresponding future locks limit	2nd Friday prior to 3rd Wed of contract mo.	$/CD $.005 intervals e.g. $.700, $.705	Premium + $125	Refer to Daily SPAN risk arrays generated by the CME.
Deutsche Mark Options-One DM Futures Contract	7:20 2:00 (2:00)	Mar Jun Sep Dec & Serial Month Options	D1 CM Calls PM Puts	.0001 = 1 pt. ($12.50/pt) ($12.50) cab = $6.25	Option ceases trading when corresponding future locks limit	2nd Friday prior to 3rd Wed of contract mo.	$/DM $.01 intervals e.g. $.40, $.41	Premium + $350	Refer to Daily SPAN risk arrays generated by the CME.
Japanese Yen Options-One JY Futures Contract	7:20 2:00 (2:00)	Mar Jun Sep Dec & Serial Month Options	J1 CJ Calls PJ Puts	.000001 = 1 pt. ($12.50/pt) ($12.50) cab = $6.25	Option ceases trading when corresponding future locks limit	2nd Friday prior to 3rd Wed of contract mo.	$/JY $.0001 intervals e.g. $.0042, $.0043	Premium + $400	Refer to Daily SPAN risk arrays generated by the CME.
Swiss Franc Options-One SF Futures Contract	7:20 2:00 (2:00)	Mar Jun Sep Dec & Serial Month Options	E1 CF Calls PF Puts	.0001 = 1 pt. ($12.50/pt) ($12.50) cab = $6.25	Option ceases trading when corresponding future locks limit	2nd Friday prior to 3rd Wed of contract mo.	$/SF $.01 intervals e.g. $.45, $.46	Premium + $400	Refer to Daily SPAN risk arrays generated by the CME.

PHILADELPHIA STOCK EXCHANGE
OPTION ON CASH

	BP	DM	SF	JY	CD	FF	ECU
Currency:	BP	DM	SF	JY	CD	FF	ECU
Contract Size:	£31 250	DM 62 500	SF 62 500	JY 6 250 000	CD $50 000	FF 250 000	ECU 62 500
Strike Intervals:	5 c	1 c	1 c	1/100 c	1 c	$\frac{1}{2}$ c	1 c
Quote	c/£	c/DM	c/SF	1/100 c/JY	c/CD	1/10 c/FF	c/ECU
Tick Size & Value	.01 c $3.125	.01 c $6.25	.01 c $6.25	.01 c $6.25	.01 c $5.00	.05 c $5.00	.01 c $6.25
Delivery Months:	March, June, September, December and first and second near term months.						
Exchange Hours:	04.30 to 14.30 and 19.00 to 23.00						
Guarantor:	O.C.C.						
Settlement on Exercise:	Expiring options settle on the Wednesday following expiration; at other times, settlement is on the fourth business day following exercise.						

LONDON STOCK EXCHANGE
OPTION ON CASH

Currency:	BP	DM
Contract Size:	£12 500	DM 62 500
Strike Intervals:	5 c	1 c
Quote:	c/£	c/DM
Tick Size & Value:	.05 c $6.25	.01 c $6.25
Delivery Months:	March, June, September, December and first and second near term months.	
Exchange Hours:	09.00 – 16.05 London time.	
Guarantor:	I.C.C.H.	

LONDON INTERNATIONAL FINANCIAL FUTURES EXCHANGE
OPTION ON CASH

Currency:	BP	DM
Contract Size:	£25 000	$50 000
Strike Intervals:	5 c	5 pF
Quote:	c/£	pf/$
Tick Size & Value:	.01 c $2.50	.01 pf DM 5.00
Delivery Months:	March, June, September, December and first and second near term months.	
Exchange Hours:	08.32 – 16.02 London time 08.36 – 16.04.	
Guarantor:	I.C.C.H.	

Appendix 3

Futures and Options: A Guide to International Regulation, Tax and Accounting

The following article* is a three part round-up of international regulation, taxation and accounting procedures for futures and options by Victor Levy of Arthur Andersen, and Eric Bettleheim, Daniel Bushner and Timothy Carey of Finley, Kumble, Wagner. The article first appeared in Futures and Options World, January–March 1987, and examines the rules in Europe, North America and the Far East.

Europe

UNITED KINGDOM

Rules

The Financial Services Act received Royal Assent on November 7 last year and will dramatically transform the structure of City regulation and will bring changes to the UK futures and options industry. The Act will become effective in stages throughout 1987 and will put in place a complex mixture of statute law, government regulation (administered by the Department of Trade and Industry (DTI)) and self-regulation by the markets and industry sectors involved in the investment business. The investments covered by the new law include virtually all forms of financial instruments including foreign and domestically traded futures and options contracts.

The Act says that, except in some exceptional cases, firms and individuals will require authorisation to engage in any investment business. Being engaged in an investment business without authorisation will be a criminal offence. Such authorisation may be obtained by direct application to the Securities and Investments Board (SIB) or by becoming a member of a self-regulatory organisation (SRO). The SIB has indicated its intention that most businesses will be authorised by a relevant SRO. For those who deal in futures and options the relevant SRO will be the Association of Futures Brokers and Dealers (AFBD).

It will not be necessary to be authorised or exempted until Sections 3 and 4 of the Act, which contain the prohibition and criminal penalties for violation of the Act, come into effect. This probably will not happen until November or December 1987, but any broker or dealer in futures and options should begin the process of becoming admitted to AFBD. In addition, investment managers who use futures and options should be aware that they will also require authorisation by the SIB or an SRO.

The AFBD has produced a handbook that includes its Rules, Code of Conduct and its Memorandum and Articles of Association. The Rules contain membership requirements, the provisions for compliance investigations, and discipline and arbitration mechanisms, and financial accounting and reporting requirements. The application for membership itself requires detailed information about the financial status of the applicant, background information about the principals of the applicant and a business plan. The Rules also govern business conduct including provisions as to the handling of clients' money.

UK-based brokers and dealers should be aware that their relationships with other members of an exchange will not invoke the conduct of business rules which require special disclosure in the exchange on which they are dealing is a Recognised Investment Exchange (RIE). The SIB is charged with the responsibility for recognising UK investment exchanges and together with the DTI will authorise foreign exchanges.

The SIB is expected to submit its criteria for approval of exchanges to the DTI this February or March. Liffe and the LCE will almost certainly be recognised as RIEs, but Gafta and the LME have yet to apply.

Taxes

The cost of options purchased by commercial users to hedge an underlying trading activity can be deducted as a trading expense for tax purposes. Also, any profits or losses made on such options contracts are taxed under Schedule D Case I as part of the trade. Financial institutions are also taxed under this case, since by definition it is their trade. Strictly speaking, these profits and losses can only be recognised for tax purposes when realised. However, the Inland Revenue has been prepared to accept the consistent application of mark-to-market or accrual accounting.

Transactions in traded options on a recognised exchange which do not form part of "trade" business are generally taxed under the capital gains tax rules, whereas options transactions on the over-the-counter market, or on exchanges not recognised by the Inland Revenue, are taxed under Schedule D case VI.

Financial futures are considered in a similar way. For hedge transactions, profits and losses are taxed under corporation tax or capital gains tax rules depending on the nature of the underlying transactions.

Accounts

As there have been no official pronouncements in the UK suggesting specific accounting treatments for financial futures and options, any accounting policy used should be chosen on the basis that it reflects most closely the underlying transaction. As such, the accounting treatment should be different for speculative and hedge transactions.

For a speculative transaction, it is generally accepted that the mark-to-market approach is the most appropriate accounting principle to reflect the economic reality. However, if a reporting entity values its short-term or other trading positions at the lower of cost or market value, futures contracts should also be valued in this way.

Accounting for a hedge position should be consistent with that for the related actual or expected cash transaction. A future contract will quality as a hedge if:

(a) its purpose is specifically identified and documented at the time it is entered into;
(b) the futures' price and the hedged asset or liability has a high degree of positive correlation, and;
(c) for an anticipatory hedge of an expected cash market transaction, which is likely to be fulfilled in the ordinary course of business.

Generally, the accounting treatment of options is consistent with that for futures.

FRANCE

Rules

The French securities industry, including futures and options dealing, is regulated by a mixture of public and private restrictions. All brokers, or agents de change, must belong to the National Brokers Association (Compagnie des Agents de Change) and follow its rules, which are endorsed by the Minister of Finance. In addition, all but one brokerage firm is a member of the new French financial futures exchange, Matif (Marché à Terme d'Instruments Financiers) which trades in French government bond futures.

The Association is run by an executive council – the Chambre Syndicale des Agents de Change which takes all decisions required to ensure the smooth running of the market and to enforce the regulations that govern the activities of members. The Commission des Operations de Bourse, whose members and chairman are appointed by the government, acts in a supervisory capacity not unlike the US Securities and Exchange Commission (SEC). In particular, it reviews the information that companies must legally provide, enforces corporate, insider information restrictions and deals with complaints.

A new law issued in July 1985 set up the framework for the creation of a financial futures market. The Matif, which began trading in February 1986, is located in the Paris Bourse (Stock Exchange) but as an entity it is separate and distinct from the Bourse. The Matif is operated and regulated by a clearing house, the Chambre de Compensation des Instruments

Financieres de Paris (CCIFP). The CCIFP is jointly owned by the Chambre Syndicale, and several insurance companies and banks.

The July 1985 law specifies that members of the clearing house may only be banks, brokers and certain types of financial houses. Only these members, who must be French or French subsidiaries of foreign entities, may deal on the Matif.

A further law was introduced in January 1986 which allows French mutual funds – SICAVs – to sell contracts on the Matif for hedging purposes and to buy contracts to close-out positions. In addition, it allows a SICAV to enter contracts other than for hedging purposes if such transactions are disclosed in its annual prospectus and open positions never exceed 100% of assets.

The January law did not specifically address insurance companies and pension funds although a new law pension funds although a new law governing these businesses should be issued in the near future. The Paris Stock Exchange expects to introduce traded options by April. One possibility is that the new options market may be on the Bourse itself and trading restricted to member brokers. However, French institutional investors will be able to trade options to exactly the same extent as futures, since the relevant law speaks of trading contracts generally.

Taxes

The taxation of futures and options in France differs for resident and non-resident companies. For resident companies gains and losses are taxed at the normal corporate income tax rates (45%) and are recognised at the date the contracts are settled. It could be argued that, for traded options, unrealised losses on outstanding contracts are tax deductible. This can be done by creating a provision for unrealised losses, but it must be stressed that this is an aggressive policy as the tax authorities are reluctant to allow such a provision as deductible, and this may require negotiation with the authorities. There is no difference between the tax treatment of hedging transaction and speculative or arbitrage business.

In the case of non-resident companies, gains on options and futures are treated as capital gains, and no withholding tax is due.

Accounts

New rules regarding the treatment of financial futures have been drawn up in France. These suggest separate tax treatment for speculative and hedge positions. A contract to hedge is defined in the same way as in the US under FASB 80.

Gains and losses on speculative contracts must be recognised immediately – on a daily mark-to-market basis – whereas for hedging they are deferred over the life of the hedge. When a hedged contract ceases to have characteristics of a hedge, gains and losses are recorded immediately.

There is no official statements regarding the accounting treatment of options but it is generally accepted that options need not be marked-to-market and gains and losses need only be recognised at time of maturity or sale. If an option is used as part of a hedging transaction, gains or losses can be deferred over the life of the hedge.

SWITZERLAND

Rules

There are currently no futures or options markets in Switzerland. However, the three largest Swiss banks together with the Zurich, Basle and Geneva stock exchanges have agreed to set up an options and futures exchange in Switzerland. A traded equity options market is expected to be opened at the beginning of 1988.

Changes in Swiss pension law and in the federal banking regulation have already eliminated some of the restrictions that previously restricted the investment behaviour of portfolio managers. But under present federal regulation, mutual funds are only allowed to invest in stocks, bonds, and "regularly traded fungible rights". This last category was added in the beginning of 1986 and a fund must receive specific government approval to utilise this provision. Although options and futures have been approved under this category, the use of such instruments by mutual funds has been strictly limited so far. This is partly because mutual funds are required to publish in their annual reports any losses incurred through hedging transactions.

Pension funds in Switzerland are regulated under the Swiss Pension Law, which has to date not included options or futures as permissible investments. Swiss banks are regulated under the Federal Banking Commission and are allowed freely to make any type of investment for their own account. Banks are permitted to use futures and options for hedging purposes for discretionary accounts.

Under Swiss law, the sale of any uncovered call or put by a bank on behalf of a customer is considered a credit arrangement between the bank and its customer. However, since there is a strict ceiling on the amount of credit a client can maintain with the bank and because the law counts the full value of the uncovered contract towards that ceiling, Swiss customers are often restricted by the prudential regulations governing Swiss banks.

Taxes

It is a fundamental principle of Swiss tax law that a company's books and records determine the income for tax purposes. The tax treatment of futures and options therefore follows the accounting principles adopted. Swiss tax laws do not provide for a separate taxation in respect of capital gains on corporations.

In the case of individuals, gains from futures and options trading are exempt from federal taxation, and six Cantons set a Capital Gains Tax and probably allow tax gains and losses to be deducted. However, gains from futures and options trading are tax exempt in the other 20 Cantons. The new futures and options market being set up in Switzerland will not be subject to withholding taxes.

Accounts

As a general rule, unrealised gains are deferred whereas losses are charged to the income statement at the time they become known and it is not acceptable to state an asset at a value higher than its cost of acquisition. As a result, gains on futures contracts should only be recognised at the time the contract is closed out or matures, and on options contracts at the time the contract is closed out, matures or is exercised or assigned.

Hedge accounting is generally permitted and financial institutions dealing in futures and options are allowed to recognise unrealised gains as well as losses, although this practice has yet to become widespread.

WEST GERMANY

Rules

Although equity options are traded on several of West Germany's eight stock exchanges, several types of institutional investors are prohibited by statute or by regulation from investing in options and futures. While equity options traded on an exchange are exempt under the Stock Exchange Act 1897 from the German gaming statutes, any foreigner who enters into any other type of options or futures contract with a German citizen does so with considerable risk of finding the contract legally unenforceable.

Other statutory restrictions on German institutions continue unchanged. German investment companies are generally excluded from trading futures and options by the Investment Companies Act of 1957. German insurance companies are restricted to trade only those investments expressly approved by statute and to date options and futures are not included.

The greatest hindrance to futures trading are the gaming statutes. Sections 762 and 764 of the German Civil Code applies to foreign currency transactions, financial, commodity and interest rate futures. These regulations have been applied by German courts even if the parties to the futures contract agree by a choice of law clause that foreign law should be applicable to the contract. As a result, such a contract is not binding on or enforceable by either party. There have been several cases in Germany where investors have been able to avoid their obligations for trading losses by relying on the statutes which are regarded as reflecting an important public policy and not as simply a technicality. Until these statutes are repealed foreigners are not secure in dealing in futures or options with most German investors or brokers.

Taxes

Income tax on futures and options generally follows the treatment in the financial statements. Profits are therefore subject to income tax at regular rates – neither futures nor options contracts are subject to a stock exchange turnover tax.

In the case of private investors, the option premium received by a writer is subject to income tax at the standard rate and any corresponding losses on the underlying asset cannot be offset against the premium income. Gains and losses arising from the disposal of an option are treated as a net capital gain according to actual tax court decisions. These capital gains are taxable if they represent short-term gains (less than 6 months) and exceed D-mark 1,000 per calendar year.

Accounts

Profits from futures and option trading are generally only recognised on a realised basis and provisions are made for unrealised losses. Unrealised losses have to be evaluated on individual positions and recognised. Hedge accounting is not normally permitted unless the terms of the hedging instrument and the underlying asset or liability are identical.

In the case of options, the buyers must capitalise the option at the original purchase price. The seller (writer) of an option has to show the premium received as a liability, and if the option has not expired at the balance sheet date, the writer has to provide for losses as a result of the possible exercise of the option.

SWEDEN

The Swedish financial markets continue to be divided into an internal and an external market by a stringent regime of foreign exchange control. Options Maklarna, the stock options market established in 1985, may soon face competition and a new market – Swedish Options Futures Exchange (SOFE) – should commence trading in January this year.

The principal difference between the two is that Options Maklarna is an electronic exchange and SOFE is based around a standard trading floor.

Under current legislation the Stockholm Stock Exchange cannot list futures or options, but this should change and it has been suggested that the Stockholm Stock Exchange may buy SOFE.

Both of these exchanges, however, are strictly limited to Swedish investors who are otherwise forbidden to trade options overseas because of foreign exchange controls. In addition, foreign investors cannot trade on these exchanges.

NETHERLANDS

The Netherlands continues to have financial markets relatively free of government restrictions and recent developments confirm that the Dutch authorities are willing to support the local options market. It has not been possible to successfully introduce an index option in the Netherlands becaue cash settled transactions violate the Dutch Gaming Statute (Article 1811 of the Dutch Civil Code). However, the Dutch Parliament has approved an amendment to the Civil Code to exempt index options. In response, the European Options Exchange aims to introduce a stock index option on January 26.

The Netherlands Securities Transactions Act and the Securities Transactions Decree came into force in May 1986 and are designed to provide better protection for the public against misleading offers and unscrupulous operators. The new law prohibits brokers to act in securities transactions unless they are made with people who regularly issue securities, deal or invest in them professionally, or the transaction is made by a licensed person. There are, however, certain exemptions, including members of US and Swiss stock exchanges. Licences are granted by the Dutch Ministry of Finance on the basis of an application that contains background and financial information on the applicant.

The EOE also hopes to list an American stock index option, although this has not yet received US regulatory approval.

North America

CANADA

Rules

Unlike US traders who are subject to a country-wide and relatively uniform system of futures regulation, Canadian traders and brokers must abide with not only nationwide laws such as the federal Grain Futures Act but also administrative regulations laid down by individual provinces. Anyone doing business on a Canadian exchange must therefore be familiar with Canadian federal law and also the various Futures Acts in Ontario, Manitoba and Quebec. And new provincial legislation such as the incoming Futures Act of British Columbia and the Securities Acts of other provinces will soon affect the way in which futures and options, particularly financial, are lawfully traded.

In addition, provincial statutes also delegate various degrees of authority to self-regulatory organisations. Canada's system of self regulation is similar to that of the US but it does not have a single self-regulatory authority such as the US National Futures Association (NFA)

For example, trading at the Toronto Future Exchange (TFE), Canada's most important financial futures centre, is regulated by the Ontario Securities Commission under the Commodity Futures Act of 1978 (Ontario Act). Such trading is also subject to the provisions of the Toronto Futures Exchange Act (1983) which gives the TFE board of directors broad, self-regulatory powers to govern the exchange. This authority, like similar powers granted in the US, is limited by the provisions of the TFE Act and the Ontario Securities Commission.

One key difference between the Canadian and US futures industry is how new contracts are approved. In the US, the Commodity Futures Trading Commission (CFTC) has exclusive jurisdiction to regulate futures and options trading, though is subject to some limitations on its control of futures and options on stocks and stock indices. In Canada each new financial future must either be registered with, or exempted from, registration by the provincial regulatory body before it can be traded in that province.

Futures and options dealers themselves are also subject to registration under either a provincial Securities Act or where applicable the provincial Commodity Futures Trading Act. Even where the Commodity Futures Act does not expressly provide for registration of futures brokers, as in Manitoba, it does require the membership of a specific market such as the Winnipeg Commodity Exchange and it gives the Manitoba Securities Commission authority to regulate the market.

Until recently foreign ownership of Canadian securities dealers was prohibited and non-Canadian firms could own only up to 10% of a Canadian securities broker. However, in acknowledging the need for Canadian firms to expand their capital base in a growing global marketplace the Ontario Securities Commission has amended the ownership rules. From June 30 this year it will be possible for foreign firms to own up to 50% of a Canadian dealer. And after June 30, 1988 foreign firms will be allowed to own 100% of a Canadian dealer. Given the pivotal role of the Ontario Securities Commission in Canadian securities regulation (approximately 80% of all securities are traded on the Toronto Stock Exchange) a relaxation of similar restrictions in other provinces should soon follow.

Generally, the rules governing investor protection in Canada are similar to those in the US. The rules governing customer suitability and supervision affect the daily operation of Canadian futures and options brokers. But Canadian regulations, particularly those in Ontario, are generally more clearly defined and stringent than those laid down by the CFTC.

Under Ontario Securities Commission rules, every futures commission merchant must have at least two fully qualified people who are Designated Registered Futures Principals. In addition, each commodity supervisor must pass the Canadian Commodity Supervisor Examination for which the Canadian Futures Examination is a prerequisite. And each branch office manager must pass all sections of the Supervisor's Examination except those related to the firm's capital.

Under Section 27 of the Ontario Act, each FCM must have written procedures for the supervision of the firm's business which are approved by the appropriate regulatory body. In addition, the names of the people responsible for overseeing these procedures must be given to the regulators. The procedures themselves must include the following:

- Guidelines on accepting new accounts
- Checking of transactions
- Regular review of correspondence
- Regular review of clients' accounts
- Control of clients' money
- Vetting of commodity salesmen, dealers and advisers
- Minimum equity level for discretionary accounts

- Frequent reviews of discretionary accounts
- A policy is required for the allocation of executed orders among component accounts within omnibus accounts
- Reviews of company trading accounts
- Reviews of the supervisory procedure itself.

Although technically these requirements do not extend beyond Ontario, in practice they affect most Canadian FCMs since almost all do some business in Ontario and use the Ontario Act as a national standard.

Another distinction between Canadian and US regulation is the Canadian customer suitability requirement. Under the Ontario Act:

"Each registrant . . . shall before accepting the account of a customer, make enquiries that . . . will enable the registrant to assess the suitability of trading by the customer in view of the markets in which the customer intends to trade, the scale of trading the customer intends to undertake, and the general financial need and objectives of the customer."

Thus a registrant under the Ontario Act is required to do more than make a cursory inquiry to determine whether a prospective customer has adequate resources to make an initial deposit to an account. Instead, before opening an account to trade futures and options, a broker must know its customer, including his ability to meet losses that may be incurred.

Moreover, an FCM may not simply rely on its initial determination of a customer's suitability. The regulations require that a dealer inquires as "frequently as is appropriate in view of the particular financial circumstances of the customer, to ensure that the initial determination continues to be accurate." A customer who has suffered significant losses may no longer be suitable for trading. Seemingly in this case, it would be incumbent on the registrant to cease doing business with that customer, or where appropriate reduce the levels of trading by the customer. Of course suitability is a subjective judgment and the line between suitability and unsuitability has not yet been defined by the Ontario or Canadian courts.

Nevertheless under the Ontario Act violations can result in fines of up to C$25,000 for companies and C$2,000 in the case of individuals, or one-year's imprisonment, or both. Although the Ontario Act does not expressly permit a customer to sue for violations of the suitability requirements it would be surprising if the private right of action is not implied. If a private right of action is implied, an "unsuitable" customer or a customer permitted to engage in unsuitable trades conceivably could avoid paying his trading debts. In fact, a customer who has suffered losses might recover his losses even if they were the result of his own folly.

Taxes

The taxation of gains or losses from transactions involving futures and options depends on the nature of the taxpayer's business, the underlying transaction and reporting method chosen by the taxpayer.

The issue of whether a gain or loss on futures or options is capital or income depends largely on the relationship of the transaction to the taxpayer's business. For example, where the trading of futures or options is connected with the taxpayer's business (such as when trading in such instruments is part of the taxpayer's regular business or the taxpayer makes hedge position on trading assets), the gain or loss is treated as an income gain or loss. In other situations, the taxpayer is permitted the option of selecting the reporting method of the gain or loss – in other words, the taxpayer can select income or capital treatment – provided the method is used consistently from year to year.

If the gain or loss is considered to be ordinary income, the full amount of the gain or loss is included in income for tax purposes. A gain or loss that is of a capital nature results in one-half of the gain being included in income and only one-half of the loss being eligible for deduction. A capital loss can only be deducted against capital gains. However, a capital loss can be carried back three years and forward indefinitely.

The treatment of a gain or loss as income or capital determines the timing of recognising the gain or loss. Generally, where the gain or loss is considered as income, it is recognised on an accrual basis. If the gain or loss is of a capital nature, then the gain it is recognised only when the contract has been closed out.

Accounts

Generally accepted Canadian accounting principles for futures and options are not currently codified. However, there does exist in practice a set of principles on the specific accounting treatment of such contracts which are followed in Canada. This accounting treatment can be broadly classified into hedge accounting and mark-to-market accounting and they are applicable to transactions involving futures and options contracts.

The gain or loss from a futures or options transaction entered into as a hedge is generally deferred, rather than recognised currently in income. The timing of the recognition of this gain or loss into the income statement would depend on the specific asset or liability being hedged. Hedge accounting treatment applies if the following criteria are met:

(a) the item to be hedged is exposed to price or interest rate risk;
(b) the position reduces the price or interest rate exposure; and
(c) the transaction is designated as a hedge at the outset of the contract.

For all transactions that do not qualify for hedge accounting – in other words, speculative positions or contracts that represent hedges of asset positions which are or will be carried at market value – mark-to-market accounting is generally employed. This principle recognises realised and unrealised gains and losses in the income statement on a current basis. As an alternative to mark-to-market, purchased options may be stated at the lower of cost or market and written options at the higher of proceeds received or market.

UNITED STATES

Rules

Futures and options trading in the US is regulated almost entirely by the Commodity Futures Trading Commission. The breadth of the CFTC authority generally extends only to trading on US exchanges. However, the Commodity Exchange Act (CEA) also empowers the Commission to regulate all transactions in the US involving commodity and future trading, whether such transactions are executed on a US exchange or not.

Thus in 1975 the CFTC promulgated regulations prohibiting fraud in the domestic offer and sale of foreign futures contracts. In 1982 amendments to the CEA significantly expanded the CFTC's authority in respect of foreign futures and options transactions to include registration, disclosure, record keeping, financial requirements and fraudulent activities.

Under recent amendments to the CEA, the CFTC has further expanded its reach over futures and options transactions undertaken by foreign traders. Partly in response to its frustration with judicial interpretations limiting the Commission's investigative powers, the Commission proposed, and Congress has now enacted, an amendment which broadens the CFTC's jurisdiction over foreign residents connected with US futures and options markets.

Under Section 102 of the Futures Trading Act 1986, the CFTC is empowered to serve and enforce its administrative subpoenas on "any person who is *not* to be found within the territorial jurisdiction" of US courts. A result is that failure to comply with an administrative subpoena served on a foreign person using the US markets may result in severe penalties.

The recent case of In re Ralli Bros (Bankers) SA, decided by the full Commission in October last year, is instructive. Ralli Brothers, a Swiss bank trading on US markets, refused to respond to "a special call" for information relating to the accounts maintained at the bank. The Administrative Law Judge who initially heard the action said that by engaging in trading on US markets the bank knew and accepted that it was subject to the CFTC's reporting requirements. On this basis, the bank was barred from US markets for two years, fined $100,000 and ordered to cease and desist from violations of the regulations. On appeal to the Commission the order was affirmed on substantially similar reasoning. The Commission, however, vacated the fine as unusually severe in light of the two-year trading suspension which the Commission upheld.

The CFTC's ability to gather foreign trading information has been further enhanced by the signing of a Memorandum of Understanding between the UK Department of Trade and Industry (DTI), the FTC and the US Securities and Exchange Commission (SEC). Under the Memorandum, the US and UK authorities have agreed to assist each other by providing information that will "enable the (recipient regulator) to secure compliance with the relevant legal rules and requirements."

The Memorandum provides for exchanges of information to prevent misrepresentation or manipulation of futures and options contracts. The agreement also establishes a general framework for information exchange while contemplating a formal and comprehensive mutual assistance treaty. Similar understandings have been reached between the US and Canada, Singapore, Australia and Japan are being negotiated.

Despite the CFTC's concern that foreign futures and options transactions can impose new and different problems for the industry, it is not without its benefits. Since 1978, CFTC regulations have banned the sale of foreign options to US citizens and residents. However, CFTC chairman Susan Phillips recently observed that "the new climate of co-operation and agreement now existing among governments and self-regulatory organisations will help (the Commission) police options activity to prevent the types of frauds" that gave rise to the options ban. Thus, last April the CFTC published proposed rules which, if adopted, will eliminate the foreign options ban and replace it with regulations governing the manner and by whom foreign options may be sold in the US.

The CFTC's proposed regulations will require registration, disclosure, limited segregation of funds and will impose capital requirements on foreign and domestic entities that solicit orders or handle funds from US residents for the purchase or sale of foreign futures and options. The CFTC will interpret "foreign futures or options contract" broadly to encompass traditional exchange traded futures and options as well as some not ordinarily considered futures such as London Metal Exchange forward contracts.

Under the regulations, a foreign broker acting in the capacity of a futures commission merchant (FCM), introducing broker (IB), commodity pool operator (CPO) or commodity trading advisor (CTA) for foreign futures or options customers would be required to register with the CFTC. But the offer and sale of foreign futures or options to producers, processors, commercial users or merchants handling the underlying commodity would be excluded. Registration with the CFTC would, ordinarily, subject the registrant to the full panoply of CFTC regulations and reporting requirements.

But recognising that foreign brokers generally do not wish to expose themselves to the general jurisdiction of US state and federal authorities, the CFTC has proposed an alternative procedure. Under this procedure a foreign broker, IB, CPO or CTA would be exempt from registration if it entered into an agreement with a US registered FCM through which foreign futures or options solicited in the US would be dealt with. The US FCM would be designated as agent for services of process from both the CFTC and US customers. A foreign broker would be prevented from accepting customer funds except through a US registered FCM on a fully disclosed basis unless it made a deposit of $50,000 with such an FCM.

The CFTC is aware that segregation of foreign futures and options customers' funds in the US would increase the cost of entering futures and options transactions on foreign exchanges. Thus the proposed rules would impose a limited segregation requirement designated to ensure that customer funds are transferred to a foreign exchange or clearing organisation. Under the proposed rule an FCM must deposit funds as belonging to foreign futures or options customers in a distinct account. These funds may be mingled with the funds of other foreign futures or option customers but not with funds segregated in respect of US market positions.

The proposed CFTC regulations also recognise the possibility of duplicative regulation in those instances where a foreign broker is subject to comparable regulation by a foreign government or self-regulatory body. In such circumstances the CFTC might exempt a person from the regulations generally or from specific requirements. It remains to be seen whether the regulatory regime of any foreign government agency or self-regulatory body will be able to satisfy CFTC requirements.

Taxes

The character of the gain or loss, capital or ordinary, recognised from the purchase, sale or exchange of a stock option is determined by the property underlying the option. Generally, options qualify for long-term capital gains treatment if they have been held for over six months. The premium associated with such an option is non-deductible capital expenditure and is not recognised until the taxpayer enters into a closing transaction, either by purchase, sale or expiration. When an option is exercised, the writer of a call increases the amount realised upon the sale of the underlying stock and the writer of a put will decrease the basis of the purchased stock by the amount of the premium. Option transactions which form part of a dealing position receive ordinary gain or loss treatment.

Transactions in regulated futures contracts and foreign currency contracts traded on a qualified exchange, so called "1256 contracts", are subject to the mark-to-market rules. These rules treat unrealised gains and losses at year-end as being 60% long-term and 40% short-term. All contracts terminated during the year receive treatment regardless of the holding period. An adjustment to basis is subsequently made for any prior year's gain or loss, taken into account by marking-to-market.

Ordinary income or loss treatment, and not capital gain or loss treatment, applies to hedging transactions involving "1256 contracts". In order to be a hedge, the transactions must be entered into in the normal course of the taxpayer's business, primarily to reduce price risk, foreign currency or interest rate risk related to property held or obligations incurred by the taxpayer.

Accounts

Financial Accounting Standards Board Statement 80 (FASB 80) establishes generally accepted accounting principles for futures contracts. Neither foreign currency futures contracts nor forward placement or delayed delivery contracts of any type are covered by FASB 80. Accounting for foreign currency futures and forwards are specified in FASB Statement 52, which covers accounting for foreign currency translation in general.

There have been no official pronouncements in the US describing the appropriate accounting treatment for forward placement or delayed delivery contracts other than foreign currency forwards. However, accounting practice in those areas largely follows the provisions of FASB 80. Accounting for options is generally consistent with the provisions of issues Paper 86–2, a non-authoritative document issued by the American Institute of Certified Public Accountants.

Accounting for all of these financial instruments is largely dependent upon whether the transaction is entered into for speculation or hedging purposes. If specific hedge criteria are met then accounting for futures, forward or option contracts (see below) is related to the accounting for the hedged item so that changes in the market value of the hedge are recognised in income when the effects of related changes in price or interest rate of the hedged item are recognised (see below).

In order for the contract to qualify for hedge accounting, the contract must be designated by the firm or entity as a hedge of identifiable assets, liability, form commitments, or anticipated transactions (see below). In addition, the hedged item must expose the firm to the risk of changes in prices or interest rates, and the contract must reduce exposure to such risk.

Risk reduction is determined on an enterprise basis for futures and forwards other than foreign currency forwards, on a transaction basis for foreign currency forwards, and on either of these bases for options.

Generally, if futures, forwards and options contracts are purchased for speculative purposes (or those that otherwise do not qualify as hedges), unrealised gains and losses that result from changes in market prices should be recognised currently in the income statement. If the firm follows lower-of-cost-or-market as its primary accounting method, it may account for speculative positions on a lower-of-cost-or-market basis.

Somewhat different results occur in the case of foreign currency future, forward or option contracts that act as a hedge of a net investment in a foreign firm whose functional currency (as defined in Statement 52) is other than the US dollar. In these instances, the unrealised gains and losses on the hedge are generally accounted for as adjustments to the cumulative transaction adjustment account which is part of stockholders' equity. This is the same account that reflects the transaction gains and losses when the financial statements of the foreign firms are expressed in US dollars.

Hedge accounting should not be used for written options unless the option is deep-in-the-money when acquired and other hedge criteria are met.

For some instruments the component economic elements of the instruments are accounted for separately. For example, the premium or discount inherent in a forward FX contract is identified at inception and accounted for separately from changes in the spot value of the contract over its life. Likewise, the premium paid on a purchased option is divided into its intrinsic value and time value components and these may also be accounted for separately.

Statement 52 prohibits hedge accounting for a forward FX contract designated as a hedge of an anticipated transaction.

Far East

HONG KONG

Rules

Regulatory responsibility for futures and options in Hong Kong falls on the Commission for Securities. The principal statutes governing futures and options trading are the Securities Ordinance, the Protection of Investors Ordinance, the Stock Exchange Unification Ordinance and the Commodities Trading Ordinance. In 1985 the Commodities Ordinance was extended to financial futures on interest rates and stock indices. The amended Commodities Ordinance allows for cash settlement for such contracts and specifically exempts them from the gaming laws.

Both the Securities Ordinance and the Commodities Trading Ordinance stipulate that under normal circumstances dealers in securities commodities and futures must be registered with the Commission. The statutory definition of a "dealer" is very broad and solicitation of institutional investors in Hong Kong usually requires registration. The statutes also require investment advisors to be registered. In addition, there are specific prohibitions against hawking commodity futures without registration and restrictions advertising or giving out documents relating to investments in certain cases.

There are also restrictions on local investment. Section 76 of the Securities Ordinance prohibits dealers from engaging in forward or options trading in securities. Nevertheless, it is possible for Hong Kong institutional investors to trade on overseas exchanges, subject to prudential controls imposed by the various regulatory bodies. Unit trusts are restricted in trading by trust deeds and by an ordinance which imposes prudential restrictions on the percentage of such investments in relation to the total assets of the trust.

Taxes

Since taxation in Hong Kong is based on a concept of territory, excepting financial institutions, gains made on transactions on futures exchanges outside Hong Kong do not fall within the scope of Hong Kong tax. Financial institutions' profits, however, may be subject to Hong Kong tax notwithstanding the source of the profits.

Corporations who are shown to be trading on Hong Kong exchanges in either commodities or futures on a regular basis, will be taxed on gains or losses at the standard rates.

If a transaction can be shown to be a hedge transaction, any gain or loss will only be taxed if the underlying transaction is of a revenue nature. Gains arising from hedges on capital items will not be taxable as there is no capital gains tax in Hong Kong.

Accounts

There have been no guidelines or statements on accounting practice in Hong Kong on futures or options. It is generally acceptable to use the accounting principles established in the UK or US.

SINGAPORE

Rules

The principal futures and options regulations in Singapore are contained in the Securities Industries Act, the Futures Trading Act, and the rules and regulations of the Singapore Stock Exchange and Singapore International Monetary Exchange (Simex). In 1984 the Singapore Gold Exchange was reorganised into Simex for the purpose of financial futures trading. The Securities Industry Act and the Futures Trading Act were both passed in March 1986.

The objective of recent legislation is to provide even greater power to the local regulatory body, the Monetary Authority of Singapore (MAS), in response to the Pan-Electric collapse. The Futures Trading Act covers only contracts based on commodities listed on Simex and is largely modelled on the US Commodity Exchange Act. Under the legislation unscrupulous trading can result in a fine of S$100,000 and seven years' imprisonment. The law also gives MAS emergency powers to step into the market if it suspects manipulation or needs to investigate any brokers or the exchange.

In order to trade in futures, and that includes soliciting or accepting any order or otherwise dealing in futures, an individual or company must obtain a licence as a futures broker or a futures pool operator. These provisions extend to all representatives of such brokers and pool operators and to trading advisors. An application must be made to the MAS and considerable financial, accounting and personal background information is asked for. The recent regulations issued by MAS under the Futures Trading Act give detailed guidance to application requirements.

Simex membership is governed by the exchange's rules and allows for three different categories of membership:

(1) a clearing member which must be a locally incorporated company or a branch of a reputable foreign firm.
(2) a corporate non-clearing member which performs brokerage functions and may trade for its own account.
(3) an individual member who acts as a floor broker or floor trader.

There is currently no traded options market in Singapore although there are indications that one is under consideration by the authorities.

There are no general prohibitions in Singapore on institutional investors investing in overseas options. However, there are a number of restrictions on particular types of institutional investors. The principal pension fund in Singapore, the Centre Provident Fund, is government operated and it does not invest overseas. Insurance companies are regulated by statute and can only trade investments from a specified list which currently does not include futures or options. Unit trusts and investment companies are restricted to dealing in Singaporean securities under the Companies Act and regulations issued by the Registrar of Companies. Banks, however, are not directly restricted in their ability to engage in futures and options except that no single investment can exceed 30% of the bank's assets.

But there is little evidence that institutions in Singapore are actually trading many options overseas. One reason for institutional reluctance may be that options, but not futures contracts, may be subject to the prohibition of gaming contracts contained in Section 7 of the Civil Law Act.

Taxes

The tax treatment differs between "traders" and private individuals.

A trader will be taxed on profits at the normal rates (up to 33%). But it is uncertain whether taxable profits are calculated using the realised basis or the mark-to-market principle. There is concessionary treatment for Simex members. Income from futures transactions traded with other Simex members, non-residents of Singapore with no permanent establishment in Singapore, branches outside Singapore of resident Singapore companies and certain offshore banking units, is granted a concessionary tax rate of 10%.

For private individuals, speculative profits are not subject to tax as Singapore has no Capital Gains Tax. For hedging transactions, the underlying transactions are considered when deciding whether or not the gains or losses are taxable.

Accounts

There are currently two pronouncements in this area. Recommended Accounting Practice 4 establishes principles for financial futures, and the Statement of Accounting Standard 20 for foreign currency transactions particularly forward transactions. Options are not covered by any standard.

Both these pronouncements introduce the concept of hedge accounting and separate the treatment between transactions entered into for speculation purposes or hedge purposes. The definition of a hedge is contained in RAP4 and coincides with the generally perceived definition.

If hedging criteria are met, the accounting treatment is that profits and losses arising from the hedged transactions should be matched with, and accounted for consistently, with the items being hedged. However, for a foreign currency transaction that acts as a hedge of a net investment in a foreign entity, gains and losses on the hedge are taken to shareholders' interests.

If the contracts are purchased for speculative purposes, gains and losses are recognised under the mark-to-market principle.

JAPAN

Rules

The environment for futures and options trading in Japan is largely determined by the regulations of the Ministry of Finance (MoF) and the individual stock exchanges, and by the strict foreign exchange control regime which restricts investments overseas.

The role of the MoF is critical because its regulations and ministerial ordinances gives much of the detail and form to the statutes passed by the Diet. As a first step in the much discussed deregulation of Japan's markets, the Tokyo Stock Exchange introduced trading in Government Bond futures in October 1985. The Osaka Stock Exchange has also announced plans to commence stock index futures trading in April, 1987.

Recent attention has been focused on whether the MoF will lift its prohibition on Japanese domestic banks and securities firms from trading directly in foreign currency and equity instruments. MoF prohibition is based on its interpretation of Japan's foreign exchange law. During the past year it has been rumoured that banks will be granted permission to handle currencies, eurodollar negotiable deposits, negotiable certificates of deposit, and some interest rate instruments, and that Japanese securities houses will be allowed to deal in US treasury bills and long-term government bonds. However futures and options trading is more complicated for securities houses than banks since, under the Japanese Securities and Exchange Act, they are limited to dealing in "securities" and there is some doubt whether futures and options can be interpreted as such.

The traditional rationale for not allowing Japanese institutions to trade in these instruments has been that they are speculative instruments. The MoF has begun studying the introduction of options transactions for negotiable securities. It has also inaugurated an unofficial forum with representatives of the securities industry to study the adoption of options transactions in Japan. As a first step, the MoF is conducting a survey of US financial instruments. It is possible that the MoF plans to have the securities and exchange law revised early in 1988, paving the way for trading financial instruments overseas.

Foreign subsidiaries of Japanese banks and securities firms trade in foreign markets but the funds for such trading are generated locally. The holding of foreign securities by institutional investors is also limited by the MoF to 10% of their assets. MoF has notified life assurance companies that it is raising the ceiling on investment portfolios for foreign securities from the current 10% to 25% of total assets. A change in percentage limitation on foreign securities and a relaxation of the foreign exchange control laws will be required before Japanese institutional investors may actively engage in overseas markets.

Taxes

Proposals now exist to reform the Japanese taxation of futures and options and they are as follows:

> Transfer tax: At present no transfer tax is levied on futures contracts, only on transfers of securities. The proposed tax reform will reduce the existing transfer tax rates on securities and impose a tax on futures contracts.
> VAT: A form of VAT has been proposed. This will only become payable if a commodity futures contract is settled by delivery. Transfers of securities and bonds, and the closing out of futures positions will be exempt from VAT.
> Direct taxes: Corporate taxpayers are subject to tax on all realised gains irrespective of classification. Individuals, on the other hand, are not liable to capital gains on the sale of securities. Thus, if a bond futures contract is settled by delivery the gain is tax free, otherwise a gain on closing out may be chargeable, although the law on this is still unclear. Gains on sale of commodity futures are fully taxable.
> If an individual is in fact a "security dealer" he will fall out of the securities exemption. At present the threshold beyond which an individual

will be considered a securities dealer is 50 buy/sell transactions involving more than 200,000 shares per annum. The new tax proposals will reduce this to more than 30 transactions involving more than 120,000 shares. The new proposals will also confirm that a gain on close out of a bond futures contract is chargeable.

These tax reforms are only proposals and may not be implemented.

Accounts

The only authoritative guideline regarding futures and options accounting comes from the accounting treatment of Tokyo Stock Exchange bond futures. The Japanese Institute of Certified Public Accountants (JICPA) has suggested the following treatment:

(1) A profit or loss should be recognised at the date of settlement of the futures contract.
(2) The existence of any material unrealised losses on futures contracts should be disclosed together with the related balance on the futures contract, as at balance sheet date, in the notes to the accounts, unless the contract has been used to hedge any risk.

AUSTRALIA

Rules

In Australia the principal laws that govern futures and options trading are the Securities Industry Act and the Futures Industry Act 1986, a Federal Act which has identical counterparts in each state. And the National Companies and Securities Commission (NCSC) and the Australian Associated Stock Exchange (AASE) are the bodies primarily responsible for regulating futures and options trading.

Recent attention has focused on the Futures Industry Act 1986, a far reaching statute requiring all futures brokers, advisors and their representatives to be licensed and to belong to a futures exchange or association. The objective of the Act is to protect clients from fraudulent practices and to provide uniform laws across the country. The legislation specifically authorises the NCSC to broaden its powers to cover the futures industry as well as the securities sector. The Act contains measures covering fraudulent practices, insider trading, market manipulation and contains rules regarding the segregation of clients' funds. The Act applies to futures contracts, eligible commodity agreements, "adjustment" agreements and options on futures. These instruments are extremely broadly defined and care should be taken in dealing in any innovative financial instrument to assure compliance under the Act.

In order to deal in futures it is necessary to obtain a licence from the NCSC. Again, the Act contains a broad definition of dealing and extends to brokers, brokers' representatives, futures advisors and advisors' representatives. Failure to be licensed may result in a fine and imprisonment. A licensee must be a member of a futures exchange or association which serves as a self-regulatory body responsible for maintenance of orderly markets, protection of clients, and day to day regulation of its members. In addition, the NCSC requires financial accounting and personal background information on individuals and principals of corporate organisations.

During legislative passage, the Futures Act provoked some controversy because of its broad sweep. Some argued that certain types of investments such as standard life insurance policies might unintentionally be caught in the definition of an adjustment agreement under the legislation. The exact implications of the new legislation will have to be worked out with time. Those soliciting investors in Australia should seek specific advice.

Taxes

Any gains or losses arising from futures contracts entered into after 19 September 1985 will probably be subject to capital gains tax although this is uncertain. It may be possible for certain transactions to be treated by the tax authorities as gaming transactions and, as such, not chargeable to capital gains tax. This is, however, unclear.

Hedge transactions, using financial futures which form an integral part of the taxpayer's business will be considered as trading, and gains and losses chargeable or allowable as appropriate. For a company trading options, gains and losses are chargeable, deductible as part of the company's usual activity.

For isolated speculative transactions in options, any gains or losses will not be taxable unless the option is sold within one year of acquisition. Any premiums paid on options by speculators will be treated as a cost for capital gains purposes.

When hedging foreign currency obligations using options, any gain arising will be taxable if the hedge relates to:

(1) a foreign currency exposure contracted after 18 February 1986;
(2) the discharge of a revenue related obligation.

Premiums on such options are deductible where the gain is taxable.

Accounts

There are no Australian standards covering futures and options accounting and the treatment followed is generally that adopted in the USA.

Index

Accounts
  Australia, in, 193
  Canada, in, 180, 181
  France, in, 172, 173
  Hong Kong, in, 187
  Japan, in, 191
  North America, in, 183, 184
  Singapore, in, 189
  Switzerland, in, 174
  United Kingdom, in, 170, 171
  United States, in, 184, 185
  West Germany, in, 175
American option
  meaning, 157
  settlement date, 159
Australia
  accounting standards, 193
  financial regulation, 191, 192
  taxation, 192

Balance sheet
  translation risk exposure, covering, 7–9
Bear spread
  trading strategy, 84, 87–90
Bull spread
  trading strategy, 80, 83–86

Call Christmas tree
  trading strategy, 122–124
Call derivatives
  table of, 125
Call option
  intrinsic value, 158
  long, trading strategy, 69–72
  meaning, 11, 157
  short, trading strategy, 73, 76–78
Call ratio backspread
  trading strategy, 116–118

Canada
  accounting principles, 180, 181
  financial regulation, 177–179
  taxation, 180
Cash settlement option
  meaning, 157
  net settlement amount, 158
Chicago Mercantile Exchange
  currency options, 66, 165

Delta
  call derivatives, 125
  curve, prediction of, 129
  definition of, 65, 139
  delta neutral and gamma negative, 151–153
  delta neutral and gamma positive, 153–155
  gamma as percentage change in, 143–145
  put and call, of, sum of, 143
  put derivatives, 126
  use of, 139–141
Delta limit
  delta positive, risk in, 57
  example, 56, 57
  meaning, 56
  size, 57

European option
  meaning, 158
  settlement date, 159

Fat tails
  meaning, 133
  problems of, 134
Financial regulation
  Australia, in, 191, 192
  Canada, in, 177–179

Financial regulation – *continued*
France, in, 171, 172
Hong Kong, in, 186, 187
Japan, in, 189, 190
Netherlands, in, 176
North America, in, 183, 184
Singapore, in, 187, 188
Switzerland, in, 173
United Kingdom, in, 170
United States, in, 181–183
West Germany, in, 174
Foreign exchange
markets, rational behaviour of, 131
overseas contract tender, 2, 3
price list denominated in foreign
currency, 4–7
risk,
balance sheet, on translation of,
7–9
definition of, 9
exposure, not covering, 9
foreign currency options, and, 10
transaction, 1–7
short or medium term position,
establishing, 57
Sweden, in, 176
Formulae
fair price, calculating, 129–133
historical volatility, calculating, 127,
128
Forward swap
risk defined by, 63–65
France
accounting treatment, 172
futures and options regulation, 171,
taxation, 172
Futures
accounting treatment, *see under*
countries
options, combined with, 49
tax treatment,
Australia, in, 192
Canada, in, 180
France, in, 172
Hong Kong, in, 186
Inland Revenue Statement of
Practice, 161–163
Japan, in, 190, 191
North America, in, 183, 184
Singapore, in, 188
Switzerland, in, 174
United Kingdom, in, 170
United States, in, 183, 184
West Germany, in, 175

Gamma
call derivatives, 125
definition of, 65, 142
delta neutral and gamma negative,
151–153

Gamma – *continued*
delta neutral and gamma positive,
153–155
percentage change in delta, as,
143–145
put derivatives, 126
shorter dated options, of, 146
time to maturity, effect of, 146–149
Gamma limit
use of, 58–60
Glossary of terms, 157–160

Hedging
balance, striking, 35
budget hedge, 45
choice of, 35
covered option writing, 42–44
cylinder option, 45
factors to consider, 151
full exposure, covering, 40–41
low/no cost option, 45
maturity, doing nothing until, 40
options, purchasing, 41–2
range forward, 45
ratio, 55, 139–141
short option position, 49
short sterling position, graph of, 35
strategy utilised, 36–39
Hong Kong
accounting practice, 187
financial regulation, 186
taxation, 186, 187

Inland Revenue
statement of practice, 161–163
International exchanges
contract specifications, 164–167

Japan
accounting treatment, 191
financial regulation, 189, 190
taxation, 190, 191

Kappa
definition of, 66

Lambda
definition of, 66
London International Financial Futur
Exchange
option on cash, 167
London Stock Exchange
option on cash, 167
Long butterfly
trading strategy, 113–115
Long call option
trading strategy, 69–72
Long put option
trading strategy, 70, 74, 75

Long straddle
trading strategy, 93–96
Long strangle
trading strategy, 94, 97–99

Margin
meaning, 158
spread, 159

Net settlement amount
meaning, 158
Netherlands
financial markets, 176

Options
American, 157
at-the-money, meaning, 12
call, meaning, 11, 157
cash settlement, 157
considerations before trading,
counterparty credit risk, 53
currencies, 53
periods forward to deal, 53, 54
requirements, 52, 53
constant monitoring of, 66
contract, 157
cost or realisable, account at lower
of, 58
covered option writing, 42–44
cylinder, 45
danger of, 47
delta, 65, 139–141
delta limit, 56, 57
early exercise, 132, 134–138
European, 158
exchange traded, 12
exercise price, 11
fair price, calculating, 129–133
foreign currency,
definition of, 11
risk, related to, 10
forward swap, 63–65
futures, combined with, 49
gamma, 65
gamma limit, 58–60
in-the-money, meaning, 11, 158
insurance, purchase as, 42
kappa, 66
lambda, 66
listed markets, on, 54
low/no cost, 45
mark to market on regular basis, 57,
58
markets, choice of, 54
maximum P + L limit, 58–60
meaning, 159
out-of-the-money,
meaning, 12, 159
pay back, purchase for, 46

Options – *continued*
over the counter,
meaning, 12
traded compared, 13–15
premium,
changes, table of, 26–34
meaning, 11, 159
paid limit, 62
payment date, 159
price factors, 55
pricing model, use of, 68
put, meaning, 11, 159
rho, 66
risk,
delta limit, 56, 57
factors, 56
options purchased, 47, 48
options sold, 47, 49–52
size limits, appropriate, 55–57
spread, 159
strike price, 11
tax treatment,
Australia, in, 192
Canada, in, 180
France, in, 172
Hong Kong, in, 186, 187
Inland Revenue Statement of
Practice, 161–163
Japan, in 190, 191
North America, in, 183, 184
Singapore, in, 188
Switzerland, in, 174
United Kingdom, in, 170
United States, in, 183, 184
West Germany, in, 175
theta, 65, 66
time value, 159
traded. *See* TRADED OPTION
trading strategies. *See* TRADING
STRATEGIES
transactions, tax treatment, 161–163
value, gradual changes in, 49
vega, 66
volatility change limit, 61, 62
wasting asset, as, 17
Overseas contract
tendering for, 2, 3
Over the Counter market
deals on, 53–55
traded options compared, 13–15

Philadelphia Stock Exchange
option on cash, 166
Portfolio analysis
computer model, 139
delta neutral and gamma negative,
151–153
delta neutral and gamma positive,
153–155

Portfolio analysis – *continued*
   today till maturity, of, 149–151
   today till tomorrow, of, 155
Premium
   changes, table of, 26–34
   meaning, 11, 159
   paid limit, monitoring, 62
   payment date, 159
Price list
   foreign currency, denominated in, 4–7
Profit and loss
   change in volatility, effect of, 61
   maximum daily, 59
   overnight, 60
Put call parity
   test, 128
Put derivatives
   table of, 126
Put option
   long, trading strategy, 70, 74, 75
   meaning, 11, 159
   short, trading strategy, 79, 81, 82
Put ratio backspread
   trading strategy, 119–121

Random walk theory
   assumptions, 130
   bid/offer spread, 130
   foreign exchange markets, rational
      behaviour of, 131
   trading size and frequency, 130, 131
Ratio call spread
   trading strategy, 103–106
Ratio put spread
   trading strategy, 104, 107–109
Rho
   definition of, 66

Settlement
   cash option, 157
   date, 159
   first date, 158
   net amount, 158
Short butterfly
   trading strategy, 107, 110–112
Short call option
   trading strategy, 73, 76–78
Short put option
   trading strategy, 79, 81, 82
Short straddle
   trading strategy, 88, 91, 92
Short strangle
   trading strategy, 97, 100–102
Singapore
   accounting principles, 189
   financial regulation, 187, 188
   taxation, 188

Spot currency
   trading in, 52
Sweden
   foreign exchange control, 176
Switzerland
   accounting treatment, 174
   financial regulation, 173
   pension funds, 173
   taxation, 174

Theta
   call derivatives, 125
   definition of, 65, 66
   put derivatives, 126
Traded option
   meaning, 12, 159
   over the counter compared, 13–15,
      53, 54
   price movements,
      day trader sheet, 33, 34
      factors, 16
      interest rate differentials, 20
      time to maturity, effect of, 17–19,
         30–32
      underlying currency,
         changes in value, 17
         current volatility of, 20
Trading strategies
   bear spread, 84, 87–90
   bull spread, 80, 83–86
   call Christmas tree, 122–124
   call ratio backspread, 116–118
   cost and profit and loss, emphasis on,
      68
   long butterfly, 113–115
   long call option, 69–72
   long put option, 70, 74, 75
   long straddle, 93–96
   long strangle, 94, 97–99
   put ratio backspread, 119–121
   ratio call spread, 103–106
   ratio put spread, 104, 107–109
   short call option, 73, 76–78
   short butterfly, 107, 110–112
   short put option, 79, 81, 82
   short straddle, 88, 91, 92
   short strangle, 97, 100–102
   synthetics, 68

United Kingdom
   accounting treatment, 170, 171
   futures and options regulation, 169,
      170
   taxation, 170
United States
   accounting principles, 184, 185
   financial regulation, 181–183
   taxation, 183, 184

Vega
call derivatives, 125
definition of, 66
put derivatives, 126
Volatility
call derivatives, 28, 29
change limit, 61, 62
currency of option, underlying,
    20
curve, shape of, 149
historical,
    calculation of, 22–26, 133
    formula for, 127, 128

Volatility – *continued*
historical – *continued*
    meaning, 22
    measure, as, 128
implied, 26–34, 61, 128, 149
intra-day, 127, 128
selling, 132

West Germany
accounting treatment, 175
financial regulation, 174, 175
gaming contracts, 175
taxation, 175